Bridging the Opportunity Gap

Bridging the Opportunity Gap

Arrey Obenson

Copyright © 2021 by Arrey Obenson.

Library of Congress Control Number: 2020924313
ISBN: Hardcover 978-1-6641-4622-8
       Softcover 978-1-6641-4621-1
       eBook 978-1-6641-4620-4

All rights reserved. No part of this book may be reproduced or transmitted in any form or by any means, electronic or mechanical, including photocopying, recording, or by any information storage and retrieval system, without permission in writing from the copyright owner.

Print information available on the last page.

Rev. date: 01/08/2021

To order additional copies of this book, contact:
Xlibris
844-714-8691
www.Xlibris.com
Orders@Xlibris.com
820607

CONTENTS

Dedication vii
Bridging the Opportunity Gap! ix
Preface xi

Chapter 1   Opportunity Trumps Challenge 1
Chapter 2   Naive Audacity 24
Chapter 3   Big-Picture Thinking 41
Chapter 4   Shared Leadership 52
Chapter 5   It Is about People 60
Chapter 6   Step Out of Yourself 66
Chapter 7   Pain of Change 71
Chapter 8   The Chaos of Success 79
Chapter 9   Bridging the Opportunity Gap 86

Index 111

DEDICATION

This work has only been achieved with the support of the many whose paths I have crossed. To the many, I express my profound gratitude. For the purpose of this work, I must name but a few who have left an indelible mark in my journey through life.

To my dear wife, Victorine (Queen) Obenson, my greatest cheerleader and most meaningful critic, who has always inspired and demanded the best of me.

To my fan club and dear sons, Asher and Eli, for whom I strive to be exemplary every day.

To Gregory and Agnes, my dear parents, who gave me the opportunity to dream and to be the best representation of the values they instilled in me and my siblings.

To the dream team of siblings—Jane, Lilian, Aretha, Philip, Lambert, Humphrey, and Blaise—whose love and support has been beyond compare.

Of course, how could I have achieved anything without the incredible expert support of my partners Christine Albrecht, Krissy Durant, Eduardo Barros, and Pedro Zaraza?

To my mentors, Desmond Alufohai, Edson Kodama, Felix Fon-Ndikum, and Terry Hurley.

To the following presidents of Junior Chamber International with whom I had the pleasure of successful collaboration:

Salvi Batlle (Catalonia), Bruce Rector (United States of America), Fernando Sanchez-Arias (Venezuela), Kevin Cullinane (Ireland), Lars Hajslund (Denmark), Scott Greenlee (United States of America), Graham Hanlon (Ireland), Jun Sup Shin (South Korea), Roland Kwemain (Cameroon), Kentaro Harada (Japan), Bertolt Daems (Netherlands), Chiara Milani (Italy), Shine Bhaskaran (India), Ismail Haznedar (Turkey), Paschal Dike (Nigeria), Dawn Hetzel (United States of America), and Marc Brian Lim (Philippines).

To the hundreds of thousands of young and not-so-young people whom I had the honor and pleasure of working with in the last two decades, thank you!

BRIDGING THE OPPORTUNITY GAP!

IT IS ALL about the opportunity as opposed to the challenges.

It is all about the solutions and not the problems.

Too often, we allow ourselves to be defined by our challenges and our problems.

Experience tells me that individuals, organizations, and corporations that focus on their challenges are defined by their challenges. They typically suffer or collapse under the weight of those challenges.

On the other hand, individuals, organizations, and corporations that focus on their opportunities are defined by those opportunities. They typically grow and flourish.

Ideas that have flourished and organizations or corporations that have endured and succeeded in transforming our lives all focus on opportunity. They are solution oriented!

If you want your idea to flourish and if you desire to change the world and strive to grow into a leader, you must be solution oriented. You must focus on the opportunity, find the silver lining in every challenge, challenge the status quo, and be disruptive!

Don't remain stuck in your past failures. Open your mind to new perspectives, and you will prevail!

It is about the opportunity—nothing but the opportunity!

Arrey Obenson

PREFACE

> The sun will first shine on those who are standing.
> —African proverb

EVERY ONE OF us is the sum total of our experiences. I am the sum total of my experiences. From an obscure country called Cameroon, I took an unlikely path going from the courtroom to the boardroom, building individuals and communities from Cape Town to Copenhagen, and from Sydney to Santa Monica. I explored the world in the most unusual of circumstances—glamourous one day and dull the next day, hopeful on some days and filled with despair on other days. With footprints in over a hundred countries, I have walked in the footsteps of Genghis Khan in the Mongolian desert to basking in the glory of the great Malian king Mansa Musa. I have braced the opulence of the rich and felt the warm humility of the underprivileged. With every encounter, in offices and homes, farmlands and the streets, I have come home with lessons—lessons that have shaped my approach to leadership and management, lessons that I must not keep to myself, lessons that I have yearned to share with the world, and lessons that I can communicate in no more compelling way than through this book.

I have therefore compiled my life experiences, a twenty-five-year journey as part of an incredible organization, Junior Chamber International (JCI). This book is not about the organization but how my life experiences informed the way I grew in the ranks of the organization, from a simple founding member of a local organization to becoming the first person of African descent to serve as the secretary general of the organization. After leading the organization for seventeen years in various capacities and taking it in a direction I'm convinced would propel it into a future that is decades ahead of its time, I am impatient to share with the world how *we*, not I . . . how *we* did it. I have also used anecdotes, people, and places that have inspired my philosophies. Nothing in this book is intended to cast any dark light on anyone that may be referenced in this book. If anything, everything about this book is intended to illuminate and stimulate the mind of the reader. Nothing in this book picks one ideology over another—everything in this book is intended to enhance every viable and sustainable ideology.

After leaving JCI, along with four of the most amazingly talented people I have known in my nearly fifty years on earth—Christine Marie Albrecht, Eduardo Carlos Barros Vasconcellos, Kristin Jane Durant, and Pedro Antonio Zaraza-Diaz—we embarked on a journey to change the world. We created this consulting firm like no other called Transformunity. The name is born out of two words that are at the core of our philosophy—*transform* and *opportunity*. At Transformunity, we harness opportunities that transform the world. In a world full of challenges, we want to help companies focus on their strengths. We are helping organizations "bridge the opportunity gap." This book is therefore not the end; it is a conversation starter. It is the beginning of another incredibly exciting adventure that I hope that every reader can join in. In the words of an African proverb that I have grown to love so much, "The sun will first shine on those who are standing." In our journey, we strive to stand with individuals, companies and organizations so they can ascend to opportunities where the sun may shine on them.

CHAPTER ONE

Opportunity Trumps Challenge

> Fear no forest because it is dense.
> —African proverb

BOARDROOMS . . . dreadful for the CEO and employees. Too often, conversations in the boardroom are filled with discussions about what is wrong with the business or organization. The sales numbers are down, membership is declining, the app is not working as planned, too much money is spent on marketing, and the website isn't effectively meeting users' needs. Too often, these board meetings that usually bring together the greatest minds of the organization end up becoming boring, long, frustrating, and unproductive.

Board meetings are meant to be productive; they should give direction to the corporation or organization. They should capitalize on the talent of the board members and should end up helping the Business or organization have a clear vision for at least a specified period of time.

Why Does This Happen?

As human beings, we are inclined to drama. In his book *Factfulness*, the late professor Hans Rosling talks about the "dramatic attention filter," stating that of all the facts we gather, our attention filter selects the most dramatic information—this makes the world look more dramatic than it actually is. We are more likely to respond to the headline announcing doom and gloom than headlines that are hopeful. The newspaper sales are better when there is a terrorist attack as opposed to news of millions of people turning out to plant trees in Ethiopia, shattering every existing world record. It may seem as if this is only happening in the larger society, but it really differs not much from the culture of small- and medium-sized enterprises, large corporations, multinational corporations, small associations, alongside international nonprofit or nongovernmental organizations.

The little gossip at the water cooler is more likely to produce more news and make the day of many than is the sale of the day. The hosting of a successful event last night is dampened by the one moment when the presentation froze for thirty seconds. The little wins made are usually overshadowed by our desire to focus on the dramatic. This human predisposition, therefore, creeps into the well-intended meaningful boardroom discussions and consequently consumes the time allocated for moving the organization forward.

Live-Changing Perspective

Sometime in July 2009, the organization I worked for was having challenges with its annual meeting that was to take place in Hammamet, Tunisia. In an emergency executive committee meeting, I was designated to go to Tunisia to help resolve the crisis, primarily because I spoke some French but also because I was from Africa and understood a little bit about the Tunisian culture—having run two international events there and also having visited Tunisia several times.

I arrived in Hammamet, Tunisia, to find a crisis of calamitous proportion. With under three months to an annual meeting that expected four thousand delegates, there was not one contract signed to secure the conference center, hotels, small meeting rooms, and other venues for ceremonies and parties. In other words, the only news that could come out of this visit was bad news, and it did. I made a call to my boss—Edson Kodama, whom I am very indebted to—and my words to him still ring hollow to me. I said, "I need $150,000 wired to me . . . no questions asked." It seemed and sounded dramatic, but it was real. I had to make payments and had no time to waste.

I spent forty-five days in Tunisia working day and night to fix the Congress that was meant to be. After working hard throughout the days, at night, I filed reports to my boss and the board of directors. At the very beginning of my trip, I highlighted the challenges I was facing and mentioned how I was addressing or going to address the challenges. Interestingly, everyone who read the reports focused on the challenges rather than the proposed solutions. Word filtered out to potential participants that the organization was in chaos, and instead of moving forward, we spent a lot of time arguing about the challenges. One night, I could vividly remember sitting in the hotel lobby with two other colleagues and arguing about who had to order the bags for participants. At some point in the conversation, a thought crossed my mind. We had spent hours arguing over a problem rather than thinking about this as an opportunity. Here was the opportunity—who cared about bags at a Congress? For too many years, a lot of money and focus had been on the quality, natures, and designs of these conference bags— so much that they almost became the defining profile of the Congress. But here we had the opportunity to change this and focus the Congress on the participants' experience and not minor issues like a bag.

Later that night, as I sat down to write my report, I resolved to focus only on the opportunities and not the challenges. My report moved away from the challenges we faced to the remarkable things we had accomplished and the huge opportunities this presented. The response to this report was amazing. Word quickly trickled out that the Congress in Hammamet, Tunisia, would be unique in its own way. While Congress was rife with challenges behind the scenes, the nearly four thousand participants had a fantastic time. It turned out to be a great success, not for the organization or the host but for the people whom the Congress was designed for—the participants, who were granted a truly remarkable experience that inspired them to come to the next Congress and the next Congress.

The Sears versus Amazon Paradox

Corporations are created based on a brilliant idea. They are typically intended to provide a service, satisfy a need, or provide a product that improves the quality of life. Likewise, organizations and associations are created driven by a cause or a mission. As corporations and organizations begin to grow, they are faced with operational challenges that begin to consume "both human and financial resources". These challenges then so vastly consume the energy of the corporation or organization that they become defined by them.

I am always fascinated by the dynamics of Sears, Roebuck & Company and Amazon. Derek Thompson concluded in his article in the *Atlantic* of September 25, 2017, that both companies were successful "as a result of a focus on operations efficiency, low prices and a keen eye on the future of American demographics." However, one will ask why Sears filed bankruptcy while Amazon is thriving. Some people have even concluded that Amazon killed Sears and other brick-and-mortar stores, but not really.

Sears was the Amazon over one hundred years ago. It capitalized on the mailing system, leveraged the power of the catalog, and became the king in the business of product delivery at doorsteps. And then it started to invest in brick-and-mortar stores. It started out with just selling watches to selling everything to everybody.

In the 1990s, Sears started losing customers to other big retail stores like Walmart and Target. It went from 40 percent of global alliances sales to 3 percent in 2017 and consequently filed bankruptcy on October 15, 2018. Amazon did not kill Sears. In an article titled "Decades of Bad Decisions Doomed Sears" in *CNN Business*, Chris

Isidore wrote, "Decades of mismanagement and poor decisions made Sears an uncompetitive afterthought to shoppers. Key among the problems was its decision to cut costs while competitors updated their stores and built up their digital businesses."

Amazon is the Sears of today. Sears failed to capitalize on the advancing digital technology just like they had done with the postal mail for catalogs. They were instead more consumed by the challenges they were facing in the company rather than the opportunities of new technology. Amazon is doing what Sears did over one hundred years ago, only they are capitalizing on the advancement of digital technology. From the online platform, they are now acquiring stores, building warehouses, and succeeding where Sears failed. Essentially, Amazon as for now is not consumed by the challenges of survival but the opportunity to expand and venture into new areas just like Sears did over one hundred years ago.

In 1952, Florence Chadwick, an American swimmer known for her prowess in open water swimming, attempted to swim the twenty-six miles between Catalina Island and the California coastline. Since it was open water swimming with the dangers of shark attacks and even drowning, she was accompanied by boats. She swam for about fifteen hours, but because there was thick fog, she could not see the coastline. At that point, she began to doubt her ability and told her team she may not be able to make it. She was cheered on, but after about an hour, she was pulled out of the water. Once on the boat, she realized that because of the fog, she could not imagine how close she was to the shoreline. She was simply a mile away. She had almost made it, but two things stood in her way—the doubt in her ability to make it and the fog that blurred her vision. A couple of months later, she attempted the swim again and made it. She was said to have kept a mental image of the shoreline in her mind, and that enabled her to achieve her goal. Later, she successfully completed the swim a couple more times.

In 1990, the Cameroonian soccer national team, the Indomitable Lions, stunned the world by defeating the cupholders, Argentina, in the opening game of the World Cup. No one would have put their bet on Cameroon, but it came to pass that Cameroon defeated Argentina. Since then, the Cameroon soccer team has not realized such a feat. The fundamental difference is that in 1990, the team was very organized and poised to do what they did best—play and win soccer games. Then came the glory, and the money and the challenges followed. Since that World Cup, the team has been plagued with mismanagement issues, and more energy is being invested in addressing the mismanagement crisis than winning a soccer game. Yet this team has players with more experience and more exposure than the 1990 team, which primarily consisted of amateur players.

In 1994, the world witnessed the genocide in Rwanda. It is said that the Hutu ethnic majority orchestrated the attack and killing of mostly the Tutsi minority. By the time the Tutsi-led Rwandan Patriotic Front defeated the Hutu-led government, over eight hundred thousand Rwandans had died, and over two million refugees had fled the country. The country faced an unprecedented humanitarian crisis, institutions had been destroyed, and the economy was in shambles. Next entered a president with a vision. Today, Rwanda is being referred to as a success story for Africa. While Paul Kagame's reign may have its challenges and people may differ with his longevity in office, he has transformed Rwanda from the ruins of bitter genocidal war to a country of reference in Africa. While the rest of the world urged him to ensure that he had a government of quotas where each of the three main tribes would occupy positions, he focused on a policy of One Rwanda—building a country that is not divided by tribes but one that aspires to be united. He could have focused on being revengeful on the Hutu majority, but instead, he focused on building a nation that was united and progressive. He focused on what united people and not what divided them. He focused on the opportunity for a country that differed vastly from the past.

Repeatedly in my experience and looking at successful athletes, individuals, corporations, and even governments, those who succeed are those who focus on their abilities and their opportunities—not their shortcomings or challenges.

In 2008, when I was charged with the strategic planning process of Junior Chamber International, without understanding how much research had gone into the opportunity gap mindset, I set out to work with stakeholders at all levels to focus the process not on the challenges but the opportunities of the organization. It is fascinating what a game changer it was!

Going into the process, the organization was struggling with its identity, its brand, and its mission. Its membership was shrinking rapidly, and in a panic, the organization was everything for everyone and nothing. It was mired in the politics of leadership and plagued with a tradition of nearly one hundred years. If we had to focus on the challenges of the organization, it could have taken us more than a chapter, so armed with an opportunity mindset, we set out to engage the membership at all levels.

I took the time to read previous strategic plans going as far back as 1984. I found out that the strategic plans were essentially a listing of the challenges the organizations faced and possible solutions to the challenges. In essence, these strategic plans were designed to address current challenges but not designed to advance the organization. They were responding to challenges and not exploring opportunities.

In order to change the narrative, we embarked on a worldwide survey of members of the nearly two hundred-thousand-member strong organization and obtained responses from close to ten thousand members. Our questions focused on an understanding of the mission, the reason people had joined and stayed in the organization—but more importantly, what they hoped to see the organization accomplish. This was the first time in any recorded history that the organization had embarked on such an extensive survey. We engaged new members, older members, past members, ordinary members, and members in leadership. An analysis of the feedback clearly demonstrated that young people had joined the organization for their own reasons and were leaving for their own reasons. It revealed that the organization had long departed from its purpose and had become an egoistic outfit where people came to acquire skills and knowledge without a desire to apply the mission of the organization.

In advance of the team of highly qualified individuals gathering to discuss the strategic plan and the future of the organization, we recommended that they read the works of Jim Collins—particularly the books *Good to Great* and *Good to Great and the Social Sector*. This was designed to stimulate thinking so that the members of the group could think beyond the organization. It was also fascinating that for the first time, we were looking at concepts that turn around good companies or great companies for that matter and applying that to a not-for-profit organization. The key message this book demonstrated was that for a company or organization to go from good to great, it needed the following:

Disciplined people: getting the right people and keeping them focused on excellence.

Disciplined thought: being honest about the facts and avoid getting sidetracked.

Disciplined action: understanding what is important to achieve and what isn't.

Here is the effect of what this accomplished. It changed the thinking from the status quo to what the organization could become. It gave the group the hope that greatness lay ahead. Almost from the onset of the conversation, the team was focused on designing a new future for the organization and not focused on troubleshooting. At the end of the deliberations, the team decided it was necessary to define what the mission of the organization was and to do so in a way that was very clear and succinct. As a result, the strategic planning committee proposed a new mission and a new vision for the organization.

The mission went from a long and wordy mission to one that was concise and succinct.

From this mission:

"To contribute to the advancement of the global community by providing the opportunity for young people to develop the leadership skills, social responsibility, entrepreneurship, and fellowship necessary to create positive change."

To this mission:

"To provide development opportunities that empower young people to create positive change."

Everything about the mission was focused on a future state, not of the organization but of what the organization could do to communities across the world. It became clear that the organization existed to create positive change, and it did so by providing development opportunities that will empower young people.

The organization also developed a vision for the first time in nearly a century of existence. The new vision projected the organization "to be the leading global network of young active citizens."

The mission and the vision were a radical departure from what the membership of the organization for several decades purported the organization to be. It was turning the focus from the individual benefits to the impact in society. It was opening the organization to the outside world by making it more relevant and allowing young people to participate in community development. Change is hard, but disciplined people lead to disciplined thought, and disciplined action will prevail.

For five years, we focused on the mission. We enforced and used the mission and vision at the start of every event and developed a plethora of material conveying the new mission. We went on the road to promote this new mission and developed sessions to explain the mission. It was an amazing feat for any organization to accomplish. Within five years across the world, in over 120 countries, the old mission disappeared and had been completely forgotten. In many instances in my travels around the world, I would test the efficiency of our strategy by asking members to recite the old mission, and in most cases, no one remembered it.

We decided to run all activities through the lens of the mission. It meant we had to decide to abandon certain programs, much to the chagrin of a small but loud portion of the membership. We could no longer afford to be everything to everybody. I became an explainer in chief traveling across the world to sell this new philosophy. I recall traveling to Lisbon, Portugal, in January 2009 to introduce the new strategic plan to the national presidents of Europe. It was a task of biblical proportions to be likened only to David going into the lion's den and coming out alive. Just imagine a man of obscure origin—Cameroon—entering a room of young and vibrant Europeans, a man eager to promote a shift from entrepreneurialism and personal development to social change and community development—to shift the focus away from egoism to instead center on impact and altruism. Armed with arguments, I made the case that the opportunity for growth of the organization was outside the walls of the room in which we sat . . . outside, where young people were yearning for an opportunity to shape their destiny. Needless to say, we prevailed, or at least I was naive enough to think so.

Life is a tale of many climbs. Every time you reach a summit, it marks the beginning of another climb. As we focused the organization on its opportunities, we were overwhelmed by the change brought by opportunity. We embarked on positioning the organization through an extensive and elaborate branding exercise. During this process, the biggest opportunity was revealed to us. Impact—that was the opportunity. Being relevant was where there was room for growth. But what on earth gave us the audacity to think that the organization had the ability to create impact? Its recent activities and programs by no means demonstrated that. If anything, the profile of membership had dropped significantly because it was only attracting those who came to take from the organization and had little or nothing to contribute. I liken this to "osmosis"—the stronger solution pulls the weaker solution. For many years, the organization had become diluted in its mission by attracting only those who needed growth to the extent that it was left with the inability to create the kind of change the world needed. Here we were, making the greatest weakness of the organization its greatest strength. We were embarking on an audacious goal of positioning JCI as the organization that would be building a mighty army of peaceful soldiers that would take on the world's biggest challenges.

We embarked on a study to find out the strengths of the biggest local organizations or chapters around the world and see why they were successful. And it revealed a framework that became the definition of how the organization had created impact in the past and how it would create impact in the future. To successfully change the paradigm of an organization to focus on its opportunity, one must identify the strengths of the organization. You do this by looking at the things that work for the organization. We discovered some incredible treasures buried within the organization. We found riches that were hardly spoken of in board meetings, events, or even in the sidelines of meetings. We found what would become the definitions of how the organization would distinguish itself from the many other membership organizations. We found what we developed and is now a registered trademark—called the JCI Active Citizen Framework.

For many years, the conversations within the organization were focused on what was wrong with the organization. It was always about members leaving, the brand being weak, the politics within the organization being ruthless, the website not working, the event being boring, and the organization not being well-known even though it had been around for one hundred years. Each time you met a member, all they spoke about were the things that were wrong with the organization and never why they were motivated to continue to serve the organization. At caucuses, all the questions posed to candidates were about how they would fix the current problems, and hardly ever did we get a question about where the organization would go in the future. How could an organization with a mission to inspire young people to change the world become sustainable when all conversations were about its inability to achieve its very mission? All energy, all talent, and all resources were driven toward a crisis rather than toward building a purposeful future for the organization.

Obviously, my experience was with a not-for-profit membership organization, but it was no different with an individual or a corporation. The only reason you enter a race is because you believe in your ability to win. Those who win races know that they have limitations. For example, the legs are too short, so they speed up the pace, or they save the sprint for the last mile. It is the same theory—if you focus on your challenges, you will be defined by your challenges.

Opportunities lead to opportunities and even more opportunities. Back to the JCI Active Citizen Framework, in our quest to find the strengths of the organizations, we found that our most successful local organizations or chapters shared several characteristics, namely:

1. They were solving a societal problem.

2. They were engaging all sectors of society.

3. They were particularly good at giving feedback to stakeholders.

This was a light bulb—it had been shining for forty years, but we could not see it because we were blinded by our passion to focus on the problems, the challenges, and not the opportunities. From Tokyo to Cologne, Greensboro to Bogotá, and Lagos to Wollongong, these characteristics prevailed, and this was what made the organization strong. This was what, in the words of Jim Collins, took JCI from "good to great." We capitalized on this opportunity and developed the framework that essentially brought tremendous value to the organization—more than anything else had in the last twenty-five years of its existence.

The Active Citizen Framework became defined as the road map to building a more sustainable future. Incredible! This came even before the world woke up to the newfound craze of sustainability. After identifying the characteristics, we peeled the onion to find out how these three characteristics came into being and here is what we developed.

For JCI local organizations or chapters to be relevant, they must have been addressing a need. A need is a societal challenge, not only one that the members of the organization deem to be important but also one that the community as a whole deems to be important. Any organization that is addressing a societal need is relevant to that society. When a chapter made of young professionals in Tijuana, Mexico, decides to address the issue of refugee settlements within the city, that chapter becomes relevant to the people of Tijuana. But how does the chapter determine that an issue is a need? It does so by engaging the people—engaging all stakeholders by way of surveys, focus groups, town hall meetings, and one-on-one engagement. The process of creating these engagements already makes the chapter relevant and even more so when there is a solution to the outcome. Using the case of Tijuana, when the chapter brings together stakeholders to discuss the issue of the refugee settlement within the city and comes up with solutions about how to train and integrate such refugees into society, it really becomes a key player in the city. Working together with local businesses, the city administration, and other civil society organizations continue to make the organization relevant. Staying committed to providing feedback, adjusting, and adapting to new realities makes the chapter more and more relevant. This process of establishing a need, engaging stakeholders, taking actions to provide solutions, and monitoring the evaluating progress is what became known as the JCI Active Citizen Framework. This is a hidden treasure within the organization uncovered by a change of perspective—from focusing on the challenges to focusing on the opportunities. From UNESCO to AIESEC, other international organizations started buying into this framework; from Dhaka to Londrina, cities started buying into this framework for their development. Suddenly, new doors opened to an organization that used to be consumed by its own hubris.

A candle lit is not meant to stand beneath the table but must be placed high up so it shines to every corner of the room. The Active Citizen Framework was a kindled candle that allowed thousands of young people to start believing in their ability to be transformational and illuminated a path to how they could bring positive change. It was fascinating to see how young people went from struggling to comprehend the concept to internalizing and totally speaking to it at every quest.

Opportunity breeds opportunity. In 2013, tasked with leading another strategic plan, this time to run from 2014 to 2018, we relied heavily on the harvesting of the seeds sown in the recent past. Again, we focused on the opportunity mindset, having seen how successful the previous exercise had been, urging the select committee to not only read one book but also read several books from the selection of books by Jim Collins. Notably, *Good to Great*, which we had discussed earlier, but also *Built to Last* and *Great by Choice*. Both books demonstrated that successful companies or organizations, for that matter, were not successful by accident but through a deliberate process. The goals of recommending this book collection to the strategic planning committee was to open their eyes to the phenomenal opportunity that the organization had if we looked beyond the confines of our obvious limitations. In the words of Jim Collins, we were asking the members of the committee to be "clock builders and not time tellers."

We also did something unique; we recommended the committee members to read a 140-page report published by the US Intelligence in 2012 that projected the state of the world in 2030. The goal of this exercise was for the committee to see the enormous opportunities that could be derived from challenging a picture of the world. This stroke of genius still gives me the shivers. This report proved to be vital in determining how the organization would position itself against the backdrop of a world that was seeing trends of mega changes.

This US Intelligence report projected that the global balance of power would be altered primarily due to rapid technological advancement, conflicts over limited resources, and growth in population especially in urban areas. Based on that report, there were going to be radical economic and political changes. The report concluded that individuals would become more powerful, government would become weaker, there would be a significant bulge in the middle class, and global conflicts would arise as a result of conflicts within states and not between states.

Since that report was commissioned, we have seen how the complexity of the civil war in Syria and Yemen brought the world to the brink of a global war. Several countries are involved in all sides of the war in these two countries. They have become proxy wars. These wars started primarily due to food and water shortages within the countries and dragged in the international community—Russia, United States of America, Turkey, Iran, Israel and Lebanon. We have also seen how activities have brought down governments by ordinary people leveraging the use of technology. In the same way, we have experienced how elections have been influenced in Europe and the United States as a result of the abuse of technology.

Why? Why will a not-for-profit membership organization of young people seek to be inspired by the challenges of the world and position itself as an organization that can overcome those challenges? Audacious, incredibly audacious . . . We did it!

It was sometime in March 2013 when this group of highly talented and extremely qualified members of the strategic planning committee trooped into Saint Louis, Missouri, in the United States. They had come from all parts of the world, but the Europeans geographically outnumbered the rest of the world. Fate and numbers just had it that way. They had come in with their various positions about what was wrong with the organization; some had been coached by "back-seat drivers" to return the organization to its past, where it focused on individual benefits and not impact on the world. Some had come with the notion that this was a business organization, and our focus must be on entrepreneurship if we had to make an impact. Others saw impact as a threat and dreaded the organization becoming a charitable giving organization. This is the beauty of the diverse world we live in. We all have different perspectives to the same challenges. We are, however, united in our desire to solve problems.

Mindful of the complexity of getting the human mind off the challenges, we offered the committee members a sweet deal. We bought rolls of brown paper and asked the committee vituperatively to opinionate themselves on the paper concerning all the things that were wrong with the organization. We gave the committee members three full hours to dump all they could on paper. They wrote and wrote and wrote. So much was wrong, and yet we had the doors open, the lights on, and a team of incredibly gifted people from all continents around the world. We then took all that was written on the brown paper and dumped it in the lobby just outside the boardroom and then gave them clean sheets of flip chart–sized paper to write out solutions to those challenges. They wrote, but less and less until they were out of ideas. Here was the phenomenal contrast. For the exercise to write out what was wrong with the organization, we gave the committee three full hours, and most of the members ran out of time writing. For the exercise to propose solutions, we gave the committee an hour, but in about half the allotted time, most of the members had run out of ideas. This was an incredible exercise and a tremendous eye-opener for the team. As humans, we are animated by the dramatic effect of challenges. The existence of a movement of young people is not to solve administrative, technical, or operational problems. Its purpose, no matter the circumstances, must remain rooted in its mission at all times. In this case—to provide development opportunities that empower young people to create positive change.

After the exercises, we focused the discussion by the committee members on the state of the world and why there was an extraordinary need for the organization to represent the voice of the people and bring solutions to the global challenges. I must confess, it was a struggle to shift the mindset from the focus on those hundreds of problems plaguing the organization to where the organization could be in the future. We asked the committee to focus on the year 2030—just as had been done in the US Intelligence agencies report—where the organization would be in that not-so-distant future.

Having the ability to paint a picture of a future state of an organization is key to changing the mindset from a status quo of challenges to a mindset of opportunities. With a vivid picture in mind, one can identify a path to that ambitious future.

Here is the picture we painted: that JCI will become the organization that unites all sectors of society to create sustainable impact by 2030. In our mind's eye, we saw JCI growing into an organization of global repute that world leaders would turn to in times of crisis to provide solutions. This was no longer just about impact; this was about bringing various perspectives together to solve the complex challenges of the world. This was obviously greatly inspired by the Active Citizen Framework that allowed young people to understand the challenges and develop the solutions in thousands of communities across the world.

Introducing the final plan to the world, we told our story—a powerfully compelling story. We affirmed the place of the organization as if we owned the space, already stating categorically that the organization would be the organization that would unite all sectors to create sustainable impact. We drew the world's attention to the fact that traditional solutions to global issues were no longer efficient and that we needed to find new solutions to age-old problems.

We challenged young people to see every challenge as an opportunity and dared them to dream of a world that was different and work toward making that dream a reality. We reminded them that our organization had survived a century because a young man—the founder—had dared to dream. He wanted "to make a citizen a better citizen," and that dream had now mobilized millions across the world who were solving problems of their communities and countries. If he could do it then without the tools we have today, how much more with the thousands of young people who are empowered and leveraging technology today?

We told a story of world that was different as a result of the work of young people—members of the organization. If young people could work toward uniting various sectors of society community after community, then we could all work toward a more sustainable future. It was putting the collaboration of all sectors of society and the center of development, and this membership organization had the audacity to take on such a role. This was it. This was the story we crafted about our future and how we were going to get there. We were going to be the organization that led the world to overcome poverty, hunger, the economic crisis that was ongoing at the time, global warming, youth unemployment, and social inequality. A membership organization of young people between the ages of eighteen and forty. Too big a dream?

This story we told in the preamble of our strategic plan sowed the seeds for a new future for the organization that was full of opportunity.

As it is said in Africa, "We had washed our hands. We could now eat with the elders." Equipped with a new long-term positioning statement, we were ready to take on the challenges of the world and become solution providers. This time, we took the plan to the people, basing it on five key words each representing a strategy. The reason for doing this was to help the thousands of members of the organization understand, relate to, and digest the strategy.

These five words represented an amazing strategic plan that was full of opportunity:

impact, motivate, invest, collaborate, connect

Key strategies:

Impact: JCI will enable communities to achieve sustainable impact.

Motivate: JCI will create an environment in which people are motivated toward positive change.

Invest: JCI will create a financial plan that invests in long-term goals.

Collaborate: JCI will bring together like-minded partners in order to expand mutual impact.

Connect: JCI will connect people, their communities, and the global society.

Nothing about these strategies focused on solving or overcoming the challenges of the organization. Before this strategy, JCI tended to "sweat the small stuff," which presented a problem for an organization destined for greatness. This strategy became a game changer. We had projected the organization into the future and positioned the organization as one that was capable—that could take on and provide solutions to Global challenges.

From 2014 to 2018, we witnessed an incredible transformation of the organization. It was not just about membership, not just about the money, but it was about impact. We became once more very purposeful. We saw brilliant ideas of impact around the world. Young people brought together all sectors of society to build a day care center in Botswana, providing care to hundreds of children while mothers went about their incredible work of family and nation building. We saw young people in Germany provide employment skills, internships, and employment opportunities for the underprivileged. We saw young people in Aleppo, Syria, lead a movement for peace, mobilizing thousands of people to work toward prosperity in a city ravaged by the ills of a civil war.

JCI became one of the first civil society organizations that adopted the Sustainable Development Goals (SDGs) in its general assembly and committed to its implementation. The organization adopted and implemented a global campaign called Peace Is Possible in line with the Sustainable Development Goal 16. This campaign mobilized over four million young people to take some form of action to advocate peace in their communities, countries, and the world on September 21, 2016. In 2017, we worked in collaboration with the Government of Sarawak, Malaysia, to host an international summit on peace, bringing together thirty-two other organizations and over seven hundred peace activists from around the world. The organization collaborated with the United Nations SDG Action Campaign to launch the Global Youth Empowerment Fund to fund youth-led initiatives aligned to the Sustainable Development Goals. This initiative funded projects from Nepal to India, the United Kingdom to Canada, Zimbabwe to Guatemala—all the while providing development opportunities that empowered young people to create positive change.

The organization grew in stature. We were invited to serve on the board of the Ban Ki-Moon Centre for Global Citizens; host an African youth development summit in the sidelines of the 6th Tokyo International Conference for Africa Development (TICAD VI) in Nairobi, Kenya, in August 2016; host an African youth development summit in the sidelines of the Mandela 100 Global Citizen Festival in Johannesburg, South Africa, in December 2018; and host an Africa youth opportunities summit in the sidelines of the 7th Tokyo International Conference for African Development in July 2019. In February of 2019, the organization was invited to join and cochair the United Nations Sustainable Development Goal's Strategy Hub Youth Stream alongside the UN Youth Envoy's office. Here, I must digress, the vision of the 2014–2018 JCI strategic plan was to see JCI one day rise to be an institution that the United Nations would turn to provide answers to the complex solutions of the world. We dreamed, and we achieved! But we did not stop there, the future was upon us, and we continued to reinvent the organization.

In 2018, we had another opportunity to design a future for JCI. Emboldened by the tremendous progress we had made in positioning JCI to be the organization that would unite all sectors of society to create sustainable impact, we felt that it was time to move the organization to the next level. Undoubtedly, we had opened the organization to new opportunities; it was now destined to create impact—positive impact. What was going to be the next move?

In the summer of 2017, a committee of incredibly talented people was appointed to serve as members of the strategic planning committee for 2019–2023. As usual, we looked for the rising stars, the experienced, and the leaders. We had an incredibly balanced committee in gender, race, religion, and experience. This time, we urged the committee members to read *Forces for Good* written by Leslie Crutchfield and Heather Mcleod Grant. This book revealed the six practices of high-impact nonprofits.

These six practices were spelled out by the authors as follows:

- Work with government and advocate for social change

- Engage the marketplace and work with businesses

- Transform your supporters into evangelists

- Treat other nonprofits as partners, not as competitors

- Adapt and innovate whenever necessary

- Empower others to lead

This book was essentially lending credit to the foundational work we had been doing in the previous ten years. Nonprofit organizations had tremendous potential to influence change, and they did so by reinventing themselves. These high-impact nonprofits worked with all sectors of society to affect social change, all the while making markets work for themselves. It was time to take the gains of the previous years to a whole new level.

After weeks of engagement remotely with the committee and three intense days of work, we arrived at the conclusion that there was a sense of urgency—that the incredible work of impact by the organization was amazing but that there was a need for accelerated action. It was themed, "Accelerate transformation." Just as we did in 2012, the strategic plan was captured in a story emphasizing to young people that the world was changing fast. Technology would connect people around the world in ways we had never imagined, and increased connectivity would create ripples of impact. In this world of heightened connectivity, governments could collapse overnight, while fortunes are made in a weekend.

With these fast changes taking place, organizations have no choice but to adapt. Organizations that do not adapt will become irrelevant and will not play a role in deciding what the future will be, especially an organization of young people like ours. We went on to say, if young people do nothing, then they will be left living in a world controlled by fear, hatred, and greed. Young people must embrace the future, a future that must be just and decisive. These young people have the power in their hands and must work together to shape the future of their communities, their countries, and the future of the world. This is how they shape their future.

To succeed, we challenged young people to work with all sectors of society and get active in the corridors of government, boardrooms of corporations, and in the streets of their communities. They—young people and members of the organizations—were called upon to be changemakers every day and, in doing so, accelerate transformation of the world.

These remarkable words were inspired by a mindset not limited by obvious challenges. This plan sets the organization to an exciting future, and only time will tell how much will be accomplished.

I told this story of my experience because it has left a powerful impression on me and, I hope, the thousands of young people who were inspired by our work. It was the United States president John F. Kennedy who said, "The problems of the world cannot possibly be solved by skeptics or cynics whose horizons are limited by the obvious realities. We need men who can dream of things that never were." This rings true today as it was in the 1960s. From climate change to income inequality, we need a mindset that is open to possibilities to find solutions as complex as they may be.

Changing from the challenge mindset to an opportunity mindset is as hard as anything that has created a meaningful transformation in human life. It is developed and enhanced with time and experience. It takes a certain level of audacity to ignore the noise and distractions of the challenges to see the opportunities of tomorrow. Sometimes it takes tremendous courage to venture into the treacherous darkness of today so that tomorrow will be as bright as the light. This courage is coined in the African proverb, which says, "Fear no forest because it is dense." After all, inside that dense forest lies the hunt for the next meal or, you can say, the next big opportunity.

CHAPTER TWO

Naive Audacity

An army of sheep led by a lion can defeat an army of lions led by a sheep.

—African proverb

I STOOD LOOKING out of the second-floor window of the office of the director of the Limbe General Hospital, Dr. Lyonga . . . lost in thoughts about what I, or we, could do to help. As I gazed down, I counted fourteen hospital wards built to provide a service to a city of nearly two hundred thousand. Gazing at the hospital wards, lined up as if they were meant to serve a military camp, I was overwhelmed by what I had just learned. None of the fourteen wards had working toilets. They were broken, clogged, no running water, and falling apart in decay. My heart ached to think that this was the place where mothers had come to have babies, and some died due to poor sanitary conditions. This was a place where patients had been brought to after highway accidents and died of infections instead of being cured. The only toilets that were working were those inside the office of the hospital director; these were the toilets used by all the nurses. I asked myself whom the hospital was meant for . . . the doctors, nurses, or the patients?

Each year, as a member of JCI Limber Atlantic, we helped the hospital, either providing bedside stools for visitors, beds, or drip stands. In 1996, serving as local president, I wanted to do something meaningful for the community hospital, and so I asked the doctor head of the hospital the one problem he would like to see solved. He took me on a tour of the hospital wards, and I discovered for myself a problem hidden in plain sight of the community. Our community hospital had no working toilets, and yet no one made it an issue. This was completely unacceptable. But I was only twenty-five years old, young, and probably naive to think I could do anything. Even more, I found out the appointed city government delegate (some sort of mayor—yes, unelected, handpicked by the government) who was a local businessman had received lots of money to rebuild the washhouses in the wards. But as was typical in unaccountable dictatorships like Cameroon, he received the money and never did the job. Taking on the solving of this problem would expose the government delegate, pit my organization against him, but profoundly affect the lives of people in the community. The benefit largely outweighed the threats.

Back at my local organization's weekly Tuesday meetings at the Victoria Guest House, I recounted my experience at the hospital. I could see in the eyes of the members that they were looking hopelessly at me and wondering if there was anything they could do. I said to them that we would renovate all fourteen washhouses. I had no idea how, but I could so clearly see the expected outcome that there was no other choice but to work toward it. Naive audacity—when you see the outcome so clearly that the odds stacked against you cannot stop you from achieving your objective.

A month later, we had put together a fund-raising gala that was intended to raise money to jumpstart the project at the hospital to renovate the washhouses. It was a flop. On the night of the event, there was a major storm that hit the city. Of the projected two-hundred people turnout, we had thirty-six people show up, mostly members of the organization. We lost money rather than raised money. I vividly remember that it was at the SS Club in Bota, Limbe. We had a visitor who was meant to be our keynote speaker, Mr. Desmond Alufohai, then serving as the director for Africa for Junior Chamber International—an incredibly motivational speaker and, full disclosure, a longtime mentor and friend. He saw in our eyes that we were beaten, and he rallied the entire audience to the dance floor and delivered a highly passionate speech about failure and success. His words that stayed with me were,

"It is only a failure if you see it that way, but if you choose to make this experience a learning exercise, then you will see it as successful."

Back at the local organization, we had to go back to the drawing board. There were the naysayers who believed this project was too big—just too audacious for a small group. There were those who were numbers driven—we had already lost money from the fund-raising gala night; why not cut the loss and run? There were those who went with the flow; they watched the debates. And then there were the dreamers—us. There was no way we could back down from such a meaningful opportunity to make a difference in the community. Hit by a strike of inspiration, I made the impassioned speech about the sign of our time. I said, "Imagine you had an accident and were unconscious and had to be taken to the nearest hospital, it probably will be the Limbe General Hospital. Imagine you're going through treatment, recovering well and dying later because of an infection due to poor sanitary conditions. All or most of us around this table can afford private medical care. If we are conscious, we will not be going to the public hospital. Now imagine how many lives we could have lost from women dying in childbirth to children dying from simple preventable infectious diseases due to poor hygienic conditions in this community hospital. If we cannot consciously seek treatment at the public hospital, how do we expect the thousands who go there to do so? They go there because they have no choice—this is what this community offers them, and this is totally unacceptable!" These words as I spoke stuck with me for the rest of my life and have become a guiding principle for me and my family.

I challenged the members of my local organization to step up and support this initiative, and after some brainstorming, we were able to come up with a brilliant idea. Take the project to the community, show people the state of the toilets, and urge them to do something about it. On our own, we could not do anything, but together as a community, we could change things. So here was what we did.

There was a trade show (Limbe Trade Fair) taking place in the city, and we decided to rent an exhibition booth in the community trade show. In booth, we displayed pictures of the hospital washhouses that were in a deplorable state. And as people came by, instead of us selling or showcasing products or artifacts as was expected, they were hit by disturbing photos of the hospital washhouses. Conversations ensued, questions were asked, some tears flowed, donations were made, and contacts were made for follow-up. After one full week of public display, we had our work cut out. A United States embassy official, whose name regretfully eludes me to this day (I hope he reads this book and learns about how his support became transformational in my life and the lives of many), gave me his business card and asked me to call him. He subsequently introduced us to someone at the British High Commission who helped us raise 25 million francs CFA (approximately 50,000 United States dollars). It seemed easy, but it wasn't. It took six months of paperwork of drafting and redrafting proposals, answering questions, adjusting budgets and financial projections, and we were also mandated to raise at least 10 percent of the project funds from the Limbe community. We raised over 10 percent; we had started a movement. We raised about 6 million francs CFA (approximately 12,000 United States dollars) from the Limbe community over nine months. Not as easy as it seemed—lots of phone calls, in-person meetings, presentations, proposals, rejections, and sometimes even threats . . . who are you to think you can do this?

Once we assembled all the money, we gave ourselves thirty days within which to complete this project. I was twenty-six years old leading a project with a budget bigger than I had ever managed and putting together a team to literally construct a new hospital. We found out that more than just the washhouses but the entire sewage system of the hospital needed a revamp. It took experts, architects, plumbers, carpenters, and electricians. We worked night and day to beat all odds to get the work done in thirty days. I was blessed with an incredible team—Cecile Ndeley, Ayuk Iyok, Julius Che Tita, Brendan Jaff (RIP), Marion Arrey, Sally Arrey, Senge Iyok, George Fonderson, Anita Mom,

Vivian Feh (RIP), Eric Takang, Lawrence Enongene, Rosemary Ebune, Stella Ndemah, Evelyne Mondoa, and hopefully, I am not leaving anyone out. This team worked incredibly hard. I am grateful.

It was March 1997, about eleven months after my visit to the hospital, that we handed and delivered to the hospital nine good as new washhouses and an entirely new sewage system. We fell short of six, but guess what, because of our engagement with the community, we sparked a movement. An oil refinery in the city called SONARA came and provided direct funding to renovate two of the remaining six washhouses. One of Africa's largest plantation agriculture corporations also came in and renovated two more, leaving two. These two were then renovated out of shame by the city government delegate, who, in his private capacity as a business owner, had failed to renovate these washhouses due to some corrupt practices they called credits. "Credits" occur when there are a budgetary allocation and funds made available for a project. It became the practice that some unscrupulous politicians and business owners colluded to expend the funds even without doing the project. Disgraced, the government delegate completed the two washhouses with the so-called credits that were left. The Limbe General Hospital now had fourteen functioning washhouses as it was meant to be. We cannot imagine the number of lives saved by this act of courage.

Looking at the odds, it was a long shot to dream of this project, but being young and foolish, we embarked on the project. Our naive audacity served as a weapon, and we did it! We were so focused on the outcome that we could not let any obstacles stand in our way. The experience was a life changer for me. It made me believe in my ability and the ability of young people to change the world.

Naive and Audacious

There is a quote from John Fitzgerald Kennedy that says, "The problems of the world cannot possibly be solved by skeptics or cynics whose horizons are limited by the obvious realities. We need men [women] who can dream of things that never were." When Kennedy came up with the idea of putting a man on the moon, whatever his inner intentions were, he certainly knew that it was a wildly outrageous idea and one that was very challenging, especially with the level of technology at the time. Because he was very clear-eyed about the outcome, he had the ability to look beyond the obvious challenges. Kennedy was not a scientist; he was a lawyer and politician. He had no idea what it would take to get a man to the moon, but he knew that it could be done if humankind set his mind to it. In fact, there was significant opposition to the moon landing. Americans were not united behind this idea. Many thought it was too expensive and that while it was a promising idea to explore the outer space, there were enough problems here on earth that demanded the use of our limited resources. Surely, there were skeptics around the President whose horizons were limited by obvious realities as to the cost, the risk, and the raison d'être. I have always been enthralled with the audacity of the moon landing speech made by President John F. Kennedy to Congress on May 25, 1961.

In the speech he made, he painted a picture of what he was asking Congress to do. He told Congress he was asking them to embark on a project that would last many years and would require the country spending billions of dollars over the next few years. He intimated that there could not be any half measures—either Congress was in or not. Coming from a politician, this was quite risky, yet he put the fate of the program in the hands of the Congress.

At this time in history, the world was going through a "race to space." The Russians had, on October 4, 1957, launched the first satellite into space, much to the chagrin of the United States. And here was the audacious President Kennedy asking Americans to not only go into space but to the moon—to be the first country to land and set foot on the moon. He wanted members of Congress to know this was a colossal endeavor. He wanted citizens to buy into the idea of going to the moon, and so he chose to appeal to the people.

For the United States to make it to the moon, a renewed commitment was needed. There had to be commitment to this project that will divert the attention of the government from the many other things that needed to be accomplished in favor of the moon landing. It meant a high level of dedication and discipline for all parties that would be involved, from the government officials to academia and contractors. Much more than money, he asked the country for a strong resolve. He demanded a pledge from civil servants, technicians, servicemen engineers, and everyone who was going to be involved in moving the space adventure forward.

The moon landing was a tall order; it was audacious. It took a certain level of naivete from the young president to believe that it was possible. It became possible. That moon landing has driven scientific progress for humankind. From advancement in flight digital controls to food safety, from space blankets to quakeproofing construction, our lives have tremendously been improved by the naivete of an audacious young man.

To be transformational, one must be able to imagine things that have never existed and bring such to reality. One must be able to see opportunity where others may not. One must be able to look beyond the challenges and be driven by the outcome rather than the process. People who are naively audacious do not need to have experience in the expected outcome. They do need to be able to clearly illustrate their vision in a way that elicits buy in from the audience. Naive audacity is what challenges status quo, leads to innovation, and changes the course of history. Ordinarily, if one weighed the obstacles against the possibility of success, one would assume impossibility, but the element of naivete motivates one's audacity.

Young people may be naive, but they are not cynical about the world. They truly believe they can change the status quo, and if that belief is exploited, it really makes a difference. It's that naive audacity in young people that fueled the Arab Spring, which changed the world in ways that we never imagined just a decade ago. Young people in Tunisia challenging the status quo imagined a Middle East that could be different. While they lacked the experience, they were naive and audacious and proved that change could happen and would happen in the Middle East. All around the world, most movements that have led to transformation have been led by young people fueled by naive audacity. Naive audacity is not experience. Young people have been criticized for their lack of experience. Examples of movements like "Occupy" and "Black Lives Matter" that originated in the United States, or "Fees Must Fall" in South Africa demonstrate that young people naively believe that they can shape the future of the world. The world is also experiencing Economic Transformation, and this transformation is led by young people. We are experiencing disruptions in the shared economy space in ways that the world never imagined. These young people are not limited by obvious realities. They are looking beyond borders, pushing the limits of technology, transforming the culture of work, and generating unprecedented profits. From the founder of WordPress, Matthew Mullenweg, to Catherine Cook, the creator of MyYearbook.com, from the creator of Mozilla Firefox, Blake Ross, to the CEO of Mashable, Pete Cashmore—these are young people who developed visions so clear that the odds stacked against them could not stop them from achieving their goals. They were naively audacious.

It almost seems like the older one gets and the more experienced one is, that sense of audacity becomes measured. Obviously, because we learn from our experiences, we appreciate the risks from our past failures rather than our successes. We become more adverse to the pain of challenges that the joy of success is obscured. One becomes more cautious and more likely to accept the status quo than challenge it. Experience makes us think through the logical steps of a process to attain our goals. Along that process, we identify obstacles. We weigh those obstacles against possible solutions, and we draw conclusions whether to proceed with an idea or not. True to our nature, we are so easily bogged down with the challenges that we lose sight of the opportunity. We lose that ability to be audacious because we are no longer naive. This by no means discounts experience, but the foregoing thesis is the reason why it is easier for young people to break new boundaries than for experienced or older people.

In June of 1992, during the United Nations Conference for Environment and Development (also known as the Rio UN Earth Summit), Severn Cullis-Suzuki, a twelve-year-old girl popularly known as "the girl who silenced the world," challenged world leaders in her speech about how our actions and our greed were damaging the planet. She sparked a movement of young environmentalists and changed the way we look at the human impact on the environment. It took a young person to be that compelling. She challenged world leaders not to break what they could not fix. This naively audacious twelve-year-old had very powerful words that visibly made world leaders uncomfortable. Even though she did not have the answers, she was convinced that we could do better as a human race or as, in her words, "thirty million species" living on planet earth. The Environmental Children's Organization, then just a group of twelve- and thirteen-year-olds from Canada who were trying to make a difference.

To get to Rio, these young children—Vanessa Suttie, Morgan Geisler, Michelle Quigg, and Severn Suzuki—had raised money to travel six thousand miles to tell world leaders to change the way they were acting. Watching her speech, you could see global leaders feel more and more uneasy as she proceeded in her speech.

What made her speech even more powerful is that as a young person, she was not motivated by a political agenda like the adults in the room. All she wanted was a future that was guaranteed. Not a future driven by the stock market or the short-term economic gains but a future in which her children and her grandchildren could still listen to birds sing. She painted. She was troubled at the way the world was going, with children dying from starvation in East Africa; animals becoming extinct; rivers and oceans being polluted, affecting the livelihood of fishermen; and air in cities becoming heavily polluted, affecting breathing.

The sheer audacity with which she made her appeal was remarkable; she said the adults did not know how to fix the world and therefore did not have to break. Even as she listed things that were wrong, she said she did not know how to fix them either, but one thing was certain: our action—human action—was causing harm to our environment, and we had to do something about it.

I have watched and read that speech over and over and over. Each time I watch, I get a moment of lucidity. In this speech, Severn Suzuki answered to the most complex challenges facing mankind. Even more fascinating is that it took a little girl to figure it out.

As part of the development of young people at JCI, we incorporated this speech as part of a course designed to inspire young people to get involved in finding solutions to the complex challenges of our time. It can be argued that this speech ignited the start of modern-day environmentalists' movements that continue to this day. But more than just the environment, she even was ahead of her time and was talking about sustainable living. She castigated greed and questioned why people in developed nations consumed so much and yet were unwilling to share with less developed nations. She spoke about wars and questioned why all the money was spent on wars around the world instead of using the money to overcome poverty.

About twenty-six years later, the world faced another awakening, this time led by a sixteen-year-old Swedish girl named Greta Thunberg, who protested for weeks in front of Parliament with a sign that read "School Strike for Climate." She has inspired a movement of young people who were skipping school to strike for the environment on Fridays. She has addressed political leaders at the United Nations, spoken to business leaders at the World Economic Forum to business leaders, met the pope, and sparred with President Donald J. Trump. Greta's naive audacity inspired the largest ever global climate strike on September 20, 2019, mobilizing over four million people. Greta is not a scientist; she has no solutions to the climate crisis but clearly understands that the pace of human activity is not sustainable for the planet. Because she is clear-eyed about her vision for a better world, she has the audacity to challenge leaders both locally and internationally to act on mitigating the impact of climate change.

Some will say she is naive. In fact, the Forty-Fifth President of the United States mocked her as having some anger management issues. He wrote in a tweet, "So ridiculous. Greta must work on her anger management problem, then go to a good old-fashioned movie with a friend! Chill, Greta, chill!" Yes, she may be naive, Mr. President, but she certainly is audacious to see that global leaders are falling short of the expectations, not because the expectations are unreachable, but because they are mired in economic and geopolitical affairs that prevent them from agreeing to tackle one of the world's biggest challenges—preserving humanity on this planet. In her naivete, Greta has the audacity to take on global leaders and to use words like she did in addressing the United Nations.

"People are suffering, people are dying, entire ecosystems are collapsing. We are in the beginning of a mass extinction and all you can talk about is money and fairytales of eternal economic growth."

She sees a problem that everyone sees but hardly anyone has the ability frame the urgency of the crisis in such a way as to spark a movement of activities that are demanding accountability of their governments. Yes, many admit climate change is a problem, but few have the audacity to commit everything possible to solve it. We start out admitting it is a problem and then immediately start seeing the obstacles about how we can solve it. We find answers to why it is not possible; we lose our naivete in the process, and consequently, we are not audacious enough in confronting the problem. We typically end up settling for the ordinary. Ordinary is not transformational. It is what has been done over and over. Ordinary achieves the expected results—ordinary!

Of course, being naively audacious does not mean one has the answers. It is the ability to imagine the alternative to the status quo and to believe in that alternative so passionately that no potential obstacles can blur out that imagination. People who are naively audacious have the ability to communicate their imagination so clearly that others can see their imagination, believe in it, and embark on its accomplishment. On their own, people who are naively audacious can hardly achieve anything. They must rely on the people around them, who become believers and implementers of the idea.

I took interest in Elizabeth Holmes, whose naive audacity took the world by storm with her invention of the Edison blood-testing device—the device that was claimed to have the ability to diagnose two hundred conditions in a few minutes from a pinprick of blood from a fingertip. What is fascinating about her story is not that she failed in her attempt to deliver on this testing device that could have revolutionized diagnostics and treatment but how much clarity of purpose she had of her vision that she was able to convince the most conservative business and global business leaders to join her board. She was so clear-eyed she created an all-star board of directors for her company, Theranos, which included William Perry (former US secretary of defense), Henry Kissinger (former US secretary of state), Sam Nunn (former US senator), Bill Frist (former US senator and heart-transplant surgeon), Gary Roughead (admiral, US navy, retired), James Mattis (former US secretary of defense, general—US Marine Corps), Richard Kovacevich (former Wells Fargo chairman and CEO), and Riley Bechtel (chairman of the board and former CEO at Bechtel Group). This was an impressive collection of men brought together by this young Stanford University dropout, whose ability to visualize her dream invention convinced them to open their wallets and networks.

At its peak, Theranos was valued at 10 billion US dollars. Elizabeth Holmes was named by *Forbes* magazine in 2015 as the youngest and wealthiest self-made female billionaire in America. She was interviewed by some of the most influential journalists of our time and had the celebrity star power. She was also named Woman of the Year by *Glamour* and received an honorary doctor of humane letters degree from Pepperdine University. Holmes was awarded the 2015 Horatio Alger Award, making her the youngest recipient in its history.

She was so focused on achieving her dreams that she did everything to achieve it—even changing her persona. It is alleged that she changed her voice to mimic that of the glorious Steve Jobs and wore black turtleneck and designer suits by Issey Miyake. She always quoted Winston Churchill, saying, "Never, never, never give up." She believed that if you could imagine it, you could achieve it.

She was naively audacious, and while she could see her dream invention, she could not figure out the complexity of the science that could make it come to reality. Faced with that complexity and intoxicated by the glamour of fame and avarice, she stretched the truth. Her invention never worked. The scheme went down in flames, and she faced several charges. Theranos completely collapsed. Elizabeth did not succeed in revolutionizing how diagnoses are made; neither did she consequently transform the way healthcare is being delivered, as was headlined. She, however, sparked a conversation around the world about the possibility of such a transformational medical testing. How did she do it? What qualities did she possess that could make her be so clairvoyant and so visionary?

It has been my experience that one must be able to drown out the cynical voices that speak from within and without. That ability is one that is cultivated and nurtured over time. No one is born with that naive audacity; people grow into it based on one of two things—a conscious effort and out of experience. Only people who have had the ability to believe in the audacity of their dreams have been able to achieve them, for without doubt, that path to every big achievement is burdened with treacherous challenges.

When a young man with an unusual name sets his eyes on the presidency of the United States, many would have thought it was a long shot. It was a long shot for Barack Obama to become president of the United States. Being black or, in reality, mixed race and having been born off the mainland in Hawaii and a name Barack Hussein Obama, the odds were insurmountable. The path to becoming president of the United States was as impossible as the biblical "camel going through the eye of a needle." And yet . . . and yet. Barack Obama is the epitome of naive audacity. He knew the odds were against him, but he could not be perturbed by them. His beliefs in what was possible for America fueled his ambition and desire to win. You could almost feel him struggle with the odds as he argued in a passionate speech about racism in America when he was accused of being very close to supposed extremist pastor Jeremiah Wright. The speech is titled "A More Perfect Union" and was delivered in Philadelphia on Tuesday, March 18, 2008. This speech probably saved his candidacy and made him president. It is a speech I recommend that every reader take interest in to understand how the odds were stacked against this man and yet his conviction in what could be possible never let him waver from his goal.

In this speech, Barack Obama painted a clear picture of why he was running for president despite the insurmountable odds—Barack Obama's ability to help people believe in what was possible. He went on to become a remarkable president for America, raising the prospects of a new future for America, or so we thought.

The pendulum swung from one side of the face of the clock to the other and brought to America and the world another naively audacious American president, Donald John Trump. Unlike President Obama, who charmed and lifted the spirits of the world with his message of change and hope, President Trump captured the dark side of Americans' deep-rooted fear of the other. A demagogue beyond compare, he was able to frame the essence of his presidency in the phrase "Make America Great Again." Love him or hate him—as you can read, I am struggling—he personifies naive audacity. Who would have expected a two-time divorcee, scandalmonger, unscrupulous crook, controversy peddler, reality TV star, and silver spoon-born millionaire to become president of the United States? Especially after the edifying tenure of President Obama. As favorably or unfavorably as you may judge President Trump, his sheer naive audacity fueled his path to the election as president of the United States.

This contrast of both American presidents is a great case study of what naive audacity is. Naive audacity as I have spelled out earlier is one's ability to visualize an outcome so clearly that it overshadows the obstacles in the way of accomplishing such an outcome. Both President Obama and President Trump were long shots from being president. They both became president with fundamentally opposing views of America and the world.

For the many years that I was in the leadership of the JCI organization, I tried hard to define my expectations of young people. What I needed of them was *naive audacity*. I wanted young people to challenge the status quo; ordinary was not good enough. Each time I imagined why our organization existed, I imagined ordinary young people doing extraordinary things. I saw in the two hundred thousand young members of JCI, a movement of two hundred thousand Severn Suzukis or Greta Thunbergs. And yet I was always heartbroken when these young people put so much energy in the process rather than the outcome. It frustrated me when people who were supposed to be reimagining the world were stuck for hours in board meetings, trying to figure parliamentary procedure, when rivers of their communities were filling up with plastic bottles and all sorts of garbage. All we wanted young people to do was believe in their ability to change the world. This is the only thing that has changed the world. People believing—yes, naively—that they can change the world is the only thing that is transformational.

I strongly believe in leading by example, even though I have been told I take on challenges too big for one man to handle. What I ask of the young people, I challenge myself to do even unconsciously. When the coronavirus continued to spread across the world, after seeing the devastating effects in Europe, as leader of the "I Am Cameroon" movement, which I will talk about later in this book, I knew like most people that the impact in Africa would be calamitous. I recalled in April of 2020 putting out a call on Facebook asking for people join me in fundraising to procure protective equipment for healthcare workers in Cameroon. When people reached out to me, I told them we needed to raise a quarter of a million dollars, and all we had to do was get 250 Cameroonians in the diaspora to put in one-thousand US dollars, and the we would provide personal protective equipment (PPE) to healthcare workers in Cameroon who were in the front line of the fight against the novel coronavirus.

Needless to say, I was naively audacious. Quickly, we put together a supervisory committee made of people who happened to show up on a virtual conference call, accepting responsibility. Swiftly, we sprung into action, unsure of our ability to raise the money. And if we raised the money, we were even unsure of how we would procure the PPE. For two weeks, I worked the phones, making contacts with people in the Cameroonian diaspora, sourcing PPE from China, Europe, and the United States. On the ground in Cameroon, we mobilized a team to engage with an association of Cameroonian private doctors and an he association Cameroonian pharmacists to identify the needs and figure out how we could support the incredible work of our miracle workers in Cameroon.

For anyone who knows the country Cameroon and knows the politics of the country, it would be insane for me, who had been denied entry into the country and harassed by the intelligence service, to still be focused on doing something big for the country, yet I knew that something had to be done, and I had to play a role in that. After all, I had spent most of my adult life asking young people to be actors and not spectators in their communities. Even though I had lived in the United States for twenty years, here I was with a conviction that will never leave me—that my home country of Cameroon can be better. Six months later, we had raised over 30,000 US dollars in cash and acquired an in-kind donation from a Japanese manufacturer of two forty-foot containers of hundreds of thousands of litres of sanitary gel worth over 500,000 US dollars to be distributed to hospitals across the country. We kicked off a fitness challenge in the month of October that mobilized the Cameroonian diaspora to keep fit, stay healthy, and support fundraising for more PPE for health-care workers in Cameroon. Naive audacity, the big things you take on because you clearly see what the outcome can be despite the enormous obstacle that stand in your way.

Across the world in big and small organizations, businesses, and communities, there are people who see challenges and see opportunities, yet their vision for action is blurred by the sheer magnitude of obstacles. They are bogged down by the process that they are unable to act. Yet only those who act make a difference. There are others who are even faced with the same magnitude of obstacles but remain unperturbed and focus on the outcome. They take one step at a time irrespective of the challenges or the failures. They try, they try, they try, and then they win—sometimes big wins, sometimes small wins. In the end, a win is a win, and naive audacity is what gives them that win.

Whether it is an athlete who wins a tournament when the odds were against her, a team that wins a championship when they aren't predicted to win, a small company that transforms the world, or a leader that emerges when pundits gave them no chance—it is naïve audacity that fuels the passion of such individuals, teams, corporations, and even countries. Naive audacity is coined in the African proverb that "an army of sheep led by a lion can defeat an army of lions led by a sheep."

CHAPTER THREE

Big-Picture Thinking

What the wise can see sitting the unwise cannot see standing.
—African proverb

"DO YOU GET the big picture?" "Can you see the big picture?" These are typical questions that we must have heard in meetings or strategy sessions. What does the big picture really mean?

The marshmallow test ID—this is an experiment that was done by Stanford University in which four- to six-year-old kids are offered the chance to have one marshmallow now or wait alone in a room with the marshmallow, not eat it, and then have two marshmallows instead after a fifteen-minute wait. As trivial as this may sound, the experiment weighs a lot on these kids who have to make the painstaking decision of forgoing short-term gain for a longer-term benefit. For most of the kids, they cave into the short-term desire for sugar and forego the second marshmallow.

The board of directors is so concerned about short-term budgetary shortfalls that they limit the hiring of staff that will support the marketing of products. An investment strategy that will yield 8 percent annually looks particularly good, but that decision will mean forgoing nonessential travel now. It will be nice to build a global reputation, but the investment in a public relations agency is too expensive. These decisions are just as agonizing as the kids' decision on whether to wait for the marshmallow. In all the examples, big-picture thinking would have led to better outcomes for the company or organization. However, the board of directors and staff are sometimes so stuck with the details of now that they fail to see what the long-term benefit of their short-term action will be.

In 2012, I was invited to speak at the International Small Business Congress taking place in Johannesburg, South Africa. This came on the heels of the launch of the JCI Active Citizen Framework, a tool designed to help organizations create sustainable impact by identifying the needs in communities and providing solutions that respond to those societal needs. In addressing the primary young business owners, I asked them to look at the big picture in going into business. Successful businesses do not just make profits. A sustainable business model is one that provides solutions to needs. Think of an app developer. No one should build an app to make money . . . yes, it should be able to make money, but that should not be the reason for the development. The reason must be that it is relevant, that it can be used to address a need or solve a problem. A corner store is not just there to sell groceries, but the only way that it grows over time is if that corner store becomes a part of the community, understanding their needs, building relationships, and making the store relevant to the lives of the people in the community. It was fascinating to see the light bulbs go on in the eyes of the young people in that room. Full disclosure, I have never really run a small business. Well, yes, I tried a sports club once, and it failed for the very reason that at the time, I wanted to make money and not build a sustainable business. I was young then. After my speech, I was swarmed by young people wanting to learn more about this big-picture thinking. I was actually struck by a conversation I had with this young woman, Glory Omoregie, who had just started a business in interior designs. In the conversation, she told me she was doing it because she was passionate about interior designs and not about the money. I asked her, "Let us see the big picture here. What will you like to achieve?" She said, "I will like for my business to be known. I want to grow my business." I took out a piece of paper, and we started a little exercise with her. I asked her why she got into this business in the first place, and she mentioned her passion. I asked her whether she was good at what she did, and she said yes. I asked her whether she would like to share her talent with someone else, and she said yes. I asked her whether she felt people would want to learn from her, and the answer was yes. I said, "Voila! This is your business model. How about instead of just having a business that does one interior decoration contract after another, you instead change to teaching people how to do interior decorations? I asked. Instead build a partnership or franchise model in which you work with the people you train to start satellites of your business in other parts of the country in order to meet growing demand. Glory's business has now grown phenomenally across Nigeria by adopting variations of a big-picture thinking strategy session.

Paul O'Niel, one time US Treasury secretary, was a big-picture thinker. His big-picture thinking, it was said, cost him his job as treasury secretary. He died recently, but he would be remembered most for the outstanding accomplishments as chief executive officer of a manufacturing company called Alcoa.

Rodd Wagner, a *Forbes* magazine contributor, wrote on January 19, 2020, that "Paul O'Neill's tenure at the helm of Alcoa is now the stuff of legend." His tenure at Alcoa is still being studied in universities across the United States.

When he was hired to serve as CEO of Alcoa, many were surprised that instead of talking in the traditional terms like that of investors and financial analysts, notably, about how he would increase profitability, bring down costs, and increase shareholder value, he instead spoke about worker safety. His vision for increasing the bottom line hinged on worker safety. It, however, takes big-picture thinking to understand that.

Paul O'Niel wanted to create a habit of excellence in Alcoa, and the way he saw it was that if the employees could be very invested in their own safety, then they would have embraced that habit of excellence. The rate of injury would then become a measure of how devoted they were to that habit of excellence. When employees embraced the company as if they owned it, they would be diligent, accidents would reduce, and the company would perform better.

As you can imagine, this made investors nervous. There were some who thought this man was crazy and pulled their investments away. However, these cynics did not see the big picture. They were looking at short-term numbers instead of long-term and sustained growth. Charles Duhigg in his bestselling book *The Power of Habit* wrote, "Someone who invested a million dollars in Alcoa on the day O'Neill was hired would have earned another million dollars in dividends while he headed the company, and the value of their stock would be five times bigger when he left."

Big-picture thinking here enabled Paul O'Neill to realize that it was the people working in the manufacturing plants who made the company successful and not the spreadsheets and investment numbers. By taking the accidents down significantly, he was able to make the company profitable. When he met with his board of directors and staff members, he always started out by talking about safety. He saw the big picture, and sure he was under the pressure of the board members, the shareholders, and the investors to show short-term results. But being steadfast and having strong convictions and the ability to communicate effectively, he pursued the transformation of the company by focusing on safety.

How Does One Develop the Ability to Think Big Picture?

You must have heard the saying, "Do not sweat the small stuff" or "Get out of the weeds." Processes enable outcomes, but processes are not the outcomes. While thinking through the process is important, getting the big picture is even more important. An association leader choosing to focus on impact rather than membership clearly delays the short-term gain of members and builds an organization that is relevant to its mission in focusing on the big picture. A chief executive officer choosing to focus on making his company a leader in climate action makes the company more socially responsible and attractive to the stakeholders that will eventually make the company and shareholders gain. A president of a country choosing to work with the international community to fight a pandemic so that the virus is contained and death significantly lowered gets it that he is protecting the lives of his own people.

No one is born with the ability to think big picture. It is a habit that is cultivated, nurtured, and allowed to become predominant in the human thought process. A habit is a process that, when repeated often, becomes part of one's subconscious. To become a big-picture thinker, one must put big-picture thinking into practice. It starts by thinking about what is wildly possible. If I asked you what is possible with the publication of this book, you will probably tell me we can sell one million copies of this book in five years. My response . . . "That's it?" How about what is wildly possible? Here is what is wildly possible—that this book becomes a reference for millions of entrepreneurs, business leaders, association leaders, and individuals around the world in bridging the opportunity gap to achieve their greatest potential. The latter perspective changes the project from just a writing and publishing project to a transformative project. The latter inspires, while the former motivates. Inspiration is an internal driving force that pushes you to achieve something, while motivation is an external force that pulls you to do something. The big picture inspires rather than motivates. The short-term gain such as a bonus, quick profits, and promotion all motivates but do not get one or a team to think big picture. When one is inspired, one is driven to stretch one's imagination to the limits. You wake up every day knowing that you are embarking on something bigger than yourself.

Here are some very simple tips.

Think about one thing that you will like to change around you. Scratch that. Think again. Think beyond yourself. This is not about you; it is not about your personal gain or happiness. What are you passionate about? What talents do you have? How can you leverage that talent to change the thing you want to change? Write these down as you go along.

Now create the space to think about what you are hoping to change. Is it providing a solution to the greatest number, or is it just satisfying your personal short-term needs? Big-picture thinking is a lot more about the greatest good.

Paint a picture in your mind of what you seek to achieve. Visualization is a powerful tool for achieving your goals. It is actually the picture in big-picture thinking.

Walk back from that big idea to where you are today and ask yourself what you have to do differently now that will create a path to that big idea.

Now it is time to take action. Do not wait for tomorrow, and do not wait to challenge the theories of this wild possibility. If the idea is too crazy to be realized, you lose nothing to have started; you only gain experience.

In 2012, I sat in a room full of some of Africa's brightest young people—or so I thought. It was the JCI Africa and the Middle East Conference Assembly. I had watched for a full day with great dismay how each leader came to speak to the room about the amazing work they had done in their various countries. All they did was praise themselves for the efforts they had done for the organization. It just did not seem like they assumed responsibility for Africa and the Middle East or their various countries. There was no big-picture thinking; it was all about themselves and the organization. I was troubled. How could it be that we bring such an outstanding group of people who were business owners, entrepreneurs, midlevel cadres, civil servants, teachers, and lawyers together—these were the people who had the capacity and ability to transform Africa, and here we were sitting in a conference room of a five-star hotel in Casablanca, Morocco, and yet outside that room were beggars asking for a meal. As Deputy Secretary General of the organization and a son of Africa, I was even more troubled.

I recall going up to the chairperson at the time, Mr. Paschal Dike from Nigeria, and asking him to allow me to address the audience. He allowed me, and I took to that podium, and to this day, I know not where those words came from. By the time I was done, I was tearing, half the audience were in tears, and everyone was on their feet, even those who did not pay attention to the words I said.

Here was my message to the young people;

> It has been 50 years and more since African countries attained independence. Fifty years ago, young people like you in this room had dreams—big dreams. They dreamed of an Africa that was free and independent, an Africa in which every child that was born had access to clean portable water, good quality education, good quality health and justice. They dreamed of a continent that had no reason to envy the West, a continent with good roads, hospitals, universities and city parks. These were young people in their late 20s and early 30s. They stood for something bigger than themselves, they were visionary!
>
> Here we are 50 years after most African countries have attained independence and yet the dreams of our founders still elude us. They gave us independence, they gave us the countries and the flags we represent in this room, now it is our time, what will we give the next generation of Africans? What will that next generation say of our generation? What were our dreams? What were our hopes and aspirations and what did we do about it?
>
> For over 50 years our organization has professed to create leaders on this continent, we have had all sorts of titles and occupied all sorts of positions and yet Africa still lags behind. We are sitting in a 5-star hotel here in Casablanca—all

dressed up in suits—and yet outside this room is a continent that is plagued with poverty, corruption, and conflict. Fifty years of trying to bring change and yet not every child that is born on the continent has access to potable water, decent quality education and access to healthcare. This is not the story of the countries we want; this is not the dream our founders had.

I challenge you my brothers and sisters to stand for something bigger than yourself, we are nothing if we are in this for self-aggrandizement, we are talking to ourselves, talking the big talk and yet we're not relevant to the people and the continent that needs us. I challenge you to be leaders not just of your National Organizations, but of your countries and of this continent that is yearning for new leadership. I challenge you to change the narrative of poverty and misery and darkness that has so plagued Africa, turn on the lights, bring hope back to your communities and countries.

I walked off that stage to rousing applause. The audience was fired up, but I knew that big picture was far from understood. Years later, my inner feeling would be proved right. Even when we can clearly see the picture, moving toward it is another challenge. I knew then, and I know now that I had to lead by example.

In December of 2012, I mobilized a group of young people in Cameroon and launched a movement called "I Am Cameroon"—in French, "Je Suis Le Cameroun." The mission of the movement is to inspire, educate, and engage Cameroonians to accept and assume responsibility for the development of Cameroon. It is, in other words, intended to help Cameroonians see the big picture. Beyond the issues that were pervasively divisive, there was a lot more that could unite us. Cameroon is a country that is suffering from the excruciating burden of its dual colonial heritage. What was meant to be a glamourous project of a unique fusion of the English (as in the United Kingdom) and French (as in France) system of governance degenerated into a project of Francophone dominance and subjugation of the Anglophones, or at least that had been the demonstrable perception.

I saw tremendous opportunity to unite the people, particularly the young people, around an idea that was bigger than the daily political sound bites. I realized that beneath the surface of a seemingly peaceful country was the boiling of anger and frustration borne by years of neglect from the ruthlessly dictatorial regime that was ruling. I knew that that pressure would explode, and I wanted to change the mindset of the people from thinking today to thinking the future—the people had become complacent and cynical about change. Corruption ran deep in the core of the country, patriotism ranked low in the people's priorities, and survival of the fittest or the most connected was the name of the game. Talking about change was met with ferocious oppression from government forces that were clamping down on any form of dissent. Yet when we introduced the movement in Cameroon, we mobilized tens of thousands of young people across the major cities of Cameroon to begin to believe in something bigger than themselves. We joined forces with other organizations to register hundreds of thousands of young people for upcoming legislative and presidential elections. We urged young people to run for office in order to bring change, and then we became a threat. As I traveled occasionally to Cameroon, since I live in the United States, little did I know that my activities were being monitored by the dreadful secret service of Cameroon. In 2016, while on a visit to Cameroon, I was accosted and interrogated for hours by the secret service in the capital city Yaoundé. They seemed not to get the big picture, or maybe they saw an even bigger picture. They had dreamed up a plan that I was going to run for president of Cameroon and had received 350 million US dollars to destabilize the government of Cameroon. You could not make this up, but it really happened. After two days of squabbles with the secret service, I departed from Cameroon, knowing we had put the story to rest. On December 21, 2017, I flew to Cameroon, and upon arrival in the economic capital, I was once more accosted by the immigration police, saying I was not allowed to enter the country. This is the land of my birth, a country... I so much loved and have been its ambassador so many years. Depriving me from entering the country was just beyond imagination. I flew back on a returning Air France flight to Paris and onward to the United States. As I am writing, I have since not returned, but the movement lives on. Since 2017, the country has degenerated into civil war, with the Anglophone regions seeking independence. This was what I was trying to avert; unfortunately, the people within the regime failed to see the big picture. After three years of bloody conflict, with over ten thousand people massacred, schools closed, hospitals burned down, and hundreds of thousands of people internally and externally displaced, the I Am Cameroon movement has still continued on its mission to inspire, educate, and engage Cameroonians to accept and assume responsibility for the development of Cameroon. As the coronavirus raged on across the world, we mobilized a few hundred Cameroonians in the diaspora to support healthcare workers in Cameroon, signing a memorandum of understanding with the second-largest health-care provider in Cameroon to help slow the spread of the virus. In spite of the fact that the people had been so divided by the burden of a needless war, they could see hope in the big picture. We had to come together irrespective of our political views to fight a common enemy—the coronavirus. I digress, but here is what the big-picture thinking looks like. It makes people imagine things that never were.

It is big-picture thinking that led to skyscrapers rising out of the deserts of the city-state known as Dubai in the United Arab Emirates. It was the vision of Sheikh Mohammed bin Rashid al-Maktoum, who saw opportunity in building an economy in the Middle East that was not solely dependent on oil. As imperfect as that vision has been, it has brought enough prosperity to the people of that nation state. Big-picture thinking is also what the small island nation of Singapore did to become one the world's biggest financial hubs. It is largely the vision and leadership of Lee Kuan Yew that led Singapore to distinguish itself from other countries like Malaysia or Indonesia that had the same socioeconomic realities at independence.

Some people have the ability to see the big picture, and others do not. I am convinced that one can train the mind as earlier mentioned to think bigger than the obvious reality. Big-picture thinking does not mean one changes the trajectory of a nation or the world for that matter, but it simply means one has the ability to see an outcome that is different from what we ordinarily obtain. Take the judiciary in the United States, for example. The aspiration of justice in the United States is "equal justice under law." Why, therefore, do politicians boast of appointing liberal or conservative judges to the courts? The notion that justice could be tilted to be favorable to the liberals or to the conservatives in my mind is in itself a conflict of the aspirations of "equal justice under law." Should we not think of the whole rather than the part? Segmenting justice into liberal or conservative divides rather than unites; it seems half of justice rather than the full. What if we just had good judges, not liberal, not conservative but good judges? Yes, this is insane thinking, but imagine how different America or the world for that matter will be if justice was justice.

The African saying, "What the wise can see sitting, the unwise cannot see standing," is sometimes elaborated on with, "The unwise cannot see even if they climb an Iroko tree." The ability to see the big picture is given to those who cultivate. Out of habit, it becomes second nature and guides decision-making and one's ability to lead, to win, and to govern.

CHAPTER FOUR

Shared Leadership

A large chair does not make a king.

—African proverb

NO ONE EVER made a difference alone. It is through developing a vision, believing in the vision, communicating that vision so clearly that others believe in it, and leading others toward the achievement of that vision. For generations, much has been invested in determining who is a leader and the different styles of leadership, so I will spare you the trouble of that. What I have not read much about is the context of leadership inspired by the African philosophy, "A large chair does not make a king."

When we think of leadership, we imagine the military general, the politician, a head of state, a statesman, a school captain, the pastor, the CEO, the boss—and I can go on and on. Our perception of leaders is usually through the prisms of the positions they hold. We are more likely to associate leadership with a title or a rank. But those attributes do not make anyone a leader. In fact, those attributes challenge anyone's ability to lead. We also visualize leadership as a hierarchical structure, where the leader sits at the top and barks down orders to the bottom, but the essence of leadership is not just giving directions. It is taking people along in a desired direction.

In the first three chapters of this book, we have focused on the opportunity mindset, the audacity of our ideas, and the ability to think big. All these cannot be realized if we do not have the ability to bring others along. Over the years, as I have played my part in societal development or occupied positions, I have grown to realize that the best way to lead people is by shared leadership.

What Is Shared Leadership?

Shared leadership as a concept has been defined and redefined in various ways, but in my opinion, Marshall Goldsmith in the *Harvard Business Review* article of May 26, 2010, attempts the closest definition to *shared leadership*. He states that shared leadership involves maximizing all the human resources in an organization by empowering individuals and giving them an opportunity to take leadership positions in their areas of expertise. Based on my experience, I have coined shared leadership to be the ability for someone in position of authority to empower others to take ownership of and apply their best qualities to the acheivement of the overall mission of the organization.

Shared leadership is not just the best way to achieve the goals of a team, in my opinion it is the only way. It demands of leaders to put their trust in others and leverage the talent of others to attain the best results for the organization. It is by no means an easy task. A leader will have to put aside his ego, step out of the spotlight, and let others shine. To do the latter, the leader must take themselves out of the equation and focus on the purpose of the organization. Will leveraging the skill sets and creating the opportunities for others to grow support the achievement of the mission?

If yes, then so be it.

I quickly learned when I was appointed to head a global organization about a condition that most leaders find themselves in. It is called the solitude of leadership. As part of an organization, you expect that everyone plays their role, and if they do so, the head goes to bed peacefully. However, that is not what is typically obtained. Leadership is mostly preoccupied with fixing those things that are broken and the systems that are not working that there is no room to drive the organization into its future. That solitude of leadership is a disease that eats you up inside as you agonize by day and by night what magical solutions you can bring to everyday challenges. The buck stops with you, the leader. Or at least it should. The shareholders, the board members, customers, and all stakeholders look to you for answers. When you are winning and lucky, a few will give you a pat on the back; when you are losing, they come down on you like a ton of bricks. Yet no one wears your shoes, no one sees or knows what you know or do not know. But the essence of leading an organization should not be solving operational problems but should be leading the organization into a future that is better than the past and present.

That "solitude of leadership," which I coined early on as a disease that everyone who has led a group must have dealt with, can become an opportunity if the leader realizes that the greatest resource in leading an organization is the people—their talent and their attitude. For this to be successful, the leader must surround himself with the right people who not only are talented but also have the right attitude and clearly understand the vision. In essence, you are not just delegating. You are sharing leadership. By delegating, you grant authority to someone to accomplish a specific task, but in sharing leadership, you grant authority and responsibility to someone to make decisions on and accomplish those tasks as if it were you doing the same. You must be prepared to assume the consequence of their decisions. You assume the failures and celebrate the success by highlighting the contribution of your coleader. The more I shared leadership, the more I could find sleep, but even more importantly, the more I could also find space for creativity, explore new horizons, and move the organization forward.

The more I pursued shared leadership, the more I could trust in the capabilities of the people on my team. In 2015, for example, I asked a fairly young teammate to chair the global celebrations of the one hundredth anniversary of my organization. This was a big deal, and I could see the shock on the faces of the members of the board of directors when I introduced to them the team lead. My trusted colleague herself did not understand that I was giving her full authority and trusting her to make decisions on the celebrations. Looking back at what we accomplished, it was phenomenal that she pulled all this together. We launched a campaign for social equality (we were way ahead of the times) and got rebuked by the board of directors, who thought that equality was not an issue—such an irony. We engaged a PR forum and started a global campaign. We launched a twenty-minute documentary, *What's in a Movement*, that was screened in hundreds of cities across the world; launched a theme song; built a hundred-thousand-dollar monument, raised over half a million dollars, and launched and sold a line of merchandise. Incredible! My colleague did not have the title of director, but she was given the opportunity to lead—and as a leader was able to steer a global organization to get a befitting one-hundredth-anniversary celebration.

Stories like this are always easier recounted after the fact than before. But they are fraught with lessons to learn. I will spare you the details of this case and share with you the lessons I learned for numerous years of implementing shared leadership.

Be Mission Driven

Occupying a position is not the reason why you're a leader. The accolades and trappings of leadership will only last as long as you are achieving the reason for which you are leading—that of the mission of the organization. Playing to the gallery and projecting yourself as a strong leader is unsustainable for the organization even if it is self-preserving for the individual. Leaders typically struggle with this notion of, "How do I protect myself in this position and yet focus on achieving the mission?" While both are not mutually exclusive, the priority must always be the mission. If self-preservation becomes the priority, then the mission invariably suffers. The organization suffers.

By focusing on the mission, one can, therefore, trust in the talent of the other members who will be advancing the mission rather than outshining the leader. If the organization is mission driven at all levels, then shared leadership becomes possible since there is alignment at all levels. As a leader, you must constantly ensure that the people you are surrounded with understand that the organization is driven by the mission and nothing else.

Communicate Effectively

Achieving the mission through leveraging the talents of the team members means that everyone on the team stays on the same page. This can only be achieved through constant and effective communication. Effective communications take various forms, and we could dwell on this for as long as the reading of this book lasts, so I will save that for another day. In my experience, there have been four ways in which I have communicated effectively with my team:

- *Be consistent.* Constantly putting the mission ahead of every conversation helps those you are sharing leadership with to understand the priorities. Being consistent on messaging at every opportunity clarifies the purpose to the team.

- *Ask questions.* Ask questions repeatedly to make sure that the goals are clearly understood. Subordinates may not feel comfortable speaking, but by asking questions, conversation is encouraged. I have been told that it could be somewhat intimidating, so this must be measured.

- *Listen.* Probably the most important skill I have acquired and that every leader must acquire is to actually listen to the people around you. Not just listen to check this box but listen, engage, debate if you have to, and take every word into consideration.

If leadership is being shared, your counterpart must also have a say.

- *Tell stories.* I have found that the most effective way of communicating is through storytelling. Probably the African in me tells me that people are intrigued by stories. Finding a story that can most effectively communicate the outcome for the team helps those who are sharing in leadership visualize the expectations. Whether it is the story of Florence Chadwick that we read earlier in this book or the biblical story of David and Goliath, use stories to help stimulate action.

Be a Collaborator

Shared leadership means this: get off the stage and take a seat in the audience. Join the team; do not just expect results. Build confidence and earn confidence in your shared leadership. Bear in mind that you want to focus on the big picture, so to do that, you must take your position out of the equation. Obviously, this may be hard for subordinates to grasp. So you must break down barriers; set the example. Here are some very simple things you can do. Make coffee for everyone during a team meeting. Offer to make notes on the flip chart. Be the last speaker on pertinent issues and only jump in if and when the conversation is losing sight of the big picture.

Be a Motivator

Sharing leadership means being a cheerleader for your shared leader. You want to see them succeed as if it were you playing the role. You are probably the best person to cheer them on. Give praise at every opportunity. Focus on the positive and highlight their strengths. There is incredible value in making someone feel trusted even when they are not performing at their best. Congratulate them on the 20 percent success they have had and focus on how you can raise the 80 percent to the standards of the successful 20 percent. As a leader who is sharing leadership, your every word and action could motivate or demotivate. Always remember that you are leveraging on the strengths of others to enhance the outcome. Harness those strengths with your words and deeds.

Celebrating Success

In January of 2019, in a bid to enhance the performance of my team, we organized a corporate retreat, and after a day of brainstorming, we found out that little things make a great deal of difference. As a team, we had achieved a lot but never gave ourselves a break to celebrate our success. We were constantly hammered by our stakeholders, rightfully so, to do more. We were always focused on putting out fires that we failed to see how much we were winning. Out of our discussion in which we took stock of just how much we had accomplished was the desire or need to celebrate our small wins. We resolved to do just that. Shared leadership entails celebrating small wins. Every milestone is worth celebrating.

Make no mistake, shared leadership is not a walk in the morning sun. It comes with its own challenges. Those challenges could be rooted in a misunderstanding of the mission, a breakdown in communication, low levels of motivation, and the precipitous burden of responsibility. Sometimes it is just a difference in expectations or the strong-willed character of the parties, but in every instance, what must reign supreme is the mission—the purpose of the organization.

As a student of shared leadership, no example has fascinated me more than the example that Nelson Mandela showed. I know you are thinking everyone celebrates Mandela, but he actually earned the accolades and exemplified the African proverb, "A large chair does not make a king." It is how you sit on it, what decisions you make while sitting on it, and how people feel with those decisions. Take away the title and the decisions will still be right, and just.

On Saturday, February 1, 1997, the *Irish Times* published the article "Buthelezi is made acting president in peace move by Mandela." Hardly do you read the headline of papers in the West about the good deeds of African leaders. It is just the way things are, so pardon me for stating this, but it was stunning that it had been published by the *Irish Times*.

Why was this headline important? Chief Mangosuthu Buthelezi, leader of the Zulu-based Inkatha Freedom Party and minister of home affairs, had been a thorn in Mandela's flesh. He was a harsh critic of Nelson Mandela's leadership and a very vocal opposition to the African National Congress, Mandela's party. Mandela was traveling out of the country to attend the World Economic Forum in Davos; he appointed Buthelezi as president of the country. This was a move that stunned most political observers. Could this be serious? However, Nelson Mandela was very serious. He saw this as an opportunity to leverage the leadership strength of his opponent to bring peace to his country. The *New York Times* wrote in its edition of February 1,1997, "For his part Chief Buthelezi, the fiery leader of the Inkatha Freedom Party, said he was filled with awe by the President's gesture and hoped nothing would happen to show that he 'did not deserve such trust.'"

It was rumored that Chief Buthelezi hardly slept in the few days of leadership as he did not want to fail in the mission that had been entrusted to him. This story best exemplifies shared leadership. Give even your harshest critic on the team the opportunity to lead. Stand by them, give them your support, and let them shine. The outcome of leveraging others' strengths only makes you a better leader for the organization and more likely to capitalize on the opportunities that lie ahead.

CHAPTER FIVE

It Is about People

Birds sing not because they like to dance but because they have songs for others to dance.
—African proverb

IN A PLUSH, almost football-sized office on the fifteenth floor of the state building in Kuching, Sarawak, I listened keenly to the chief minister of Sarawak, Abang Abdul Rahman Zohari Abang Openg, as he spoke about his dreams not for himself but for the people of his state. Sarawak is a semiautonomous state in the country of Malaysia. It is known for its rich oil and rich fauna and flora. Little is known about its people, who are peace loving and a clear example of how diverse people can live together in harmony. From the chief minister, I learned that there is a Catholic church across the street from a mosque and that on Fridays, the parking lot of the Catholic church is used by the mosque, and on Sundays, the parking lot of the mosque is used by the church. The population of Sarawak is made of people from varying ethnic groups, various religious backgrounds, and diverse languages—yet they peacefully coexist. I was fascinated by my conversation with the chief minister because he was extremely focused on how he could make life better for his people. He was anxious to promote tourism in Kuching so he could create employment for his people, but even more interesting was the fact that he wanted to build an economy that was no longer dependent on oil but agriculture. He said this may not happen in his lifetime and may not be the politically expedient thing to do, but it was the best thing to do for his people. He went on about the negative impact of fossil fuels on the climate even though the economy of his state largely depended on it.

I had traveled to meet the chief minister with a goal to explore the possibility of collaborating to host and international conference on peace. I had left the office understanding that the greatest opportunity we have on planet earth is protecting, preserving, and providing for the lives of people on planet earth. I have been lucky to travel to over one hundred countries across the planet. I have met with thousands of local leaders, from mayors to city councilors. I have met with national leaders from legislators to heads of states. I have met with business leaders from janitors to CEOs and community leaders and from activists to association heads. And in all my interactions, I have concluded that we exist for one reason: to preserve life. From the days when early man roamed the wild and lived in caves, it has always been about protecting one's life and the lives of loved ones. As we assume responsibility for our family, for a group, association, company, community, or country, our first responsibility becomes that of protecting our people.

The people we work with and the people we work for. The customer we serve and the public or community in which we operate and then our shareholders or board members as the case may be.

The reason why organizations, whether corporations or associations, exist is typically to provide a service that is relevant to people. Leaders emerge in organizations to serve people—a fundamental aspect of every organization, big or small. Typically, this is understood until other interests get in the way. Take, for example, the politician who is known by friends and family to be a good person but, upon running for office, becomes beholden to donors whose interest may not necessarily be the people the politician serves. This same scenario plagues board rooms of companies, where the CEO puts people first, and the board of directors put shareholders and, consequently, profits first. Similarly, this plays out in associations and even religious institutions, where the interest of "back-seat drivers" prevails over rational judgment to serve the membership. Why does this happen?

Education or the lack thereof. Education, the Informal or formal. The first form of education comes from the home or family in which we are born, where our core values were instilled in us. As we grow up and begin to receive a formal education, we begin to develop values that typically teach us how to live in a civilized society and is supposed to focus on how we care for one another. This foundational education is hopefully intended to define who we are. As life happens and we begin to undertake the unimaginable dreams of our early years, we seem to rationalize why those foundational values no longer matter. Our values are compromised by our interest and the interests of those around us. We start seeing wrong as right and right as wrong, or as someone put it to me, there is a wrong that is right and right that is wrong—awfully referring to the dropping of the atomic bomb. I digress. How do we explain that an association whose secondary purposes is to provide good-quality services to its members is not willing to direct resources toward incentivizing employees or hiring more employees? Instead, faced with falling membership and dwindling resources, they will rather reduce employee compensation, freeze hiring, and hope for improved quality of service. Hope is not a strategy.

As the leader of an organization, I chose the opposite path, much to the opposition of a board of directors beholden not to interests of those that elected them but to the interest of the invisible heads that give them a nod to run and be elected. Against incredible odds, we mobilized the organization to increase membership fees as a way to stimulate revenue and, after a three-year fight, saw membership fees increase for the first time in twenty years. We then embarked on the well-being of the people who were expected to provide the service as well as increased the capacity of the people in talent and numbers. We completely transformed the structure of the organization to empower the team members, understanding the strength of each person in the team and giving them more authority. As a leader, I removed myself from being the center of authority to allowing the team to lead where they were. Such forward-thinking, people-centered focus is usually seen as radical and unsettling for those who are stuck to old ways and cannot broaden their perspective. What does this mean? Change threatens interests. That decentralized power means access to power is limited and uncontrolled, even if the decentralization leads to increased output for the organization. People rationalize the status quo even against their own core values. People ignore a positive outcome if that outcome poses a perceived threat to their interest.

During the Great Depression, J. W. and Alice Marriott, founders of Marriott International, instead of laying employees off, had hired a staff doctor to take care of their people. Rasmus Hougaard, in a *Forbes* article on March 5, 2019, titled "The Power of Putting People First," writes extensively about the exemplary people-centric philosophy of J. W. and Alice Marriott, who believed that "if we take care of our people, they will take care of our customers, and the customers will come back." The founders of Marriott International went against the conventional wisdom at the time and invested in their people with the belief that if they cared for their employees and in return get a reliable, healthy workforce and if their employees had access to good medical care, they would be able to provide the level of service they wanted for their customers. Of course, Marriott International with its people-centric philosophy has withstood the test of time to become one of the largest hotel chains in the world.

The Marriotts of the world are few, but their growth and survival are testimony of the philosophy that laid the foundation of such a company. Starting out modestly as a root beer company in Washington, DC, the company has flourished by putting people at the center of what they do. Whether it is a business small or big or even an individual or an association, your existence largely depends on people—the people you serve and the people who serve you, all of whom are crucial to your survival.

Over the years, I have served as a mentor to many who typically called me when they were about to make big decisions in life. I have also had one question I always asked, Why do you want to do it? I recall a good friend, Angelica Lam from Panama called me sometime in 2014 to express her desire to run for national president for her JCI organization. Being national president was seen as prestigious. You earn the respect and sometimes adoration of many. You also get the opportunity to make decisions that will help develop the organization within the country. It was and still is a position that can make a difference not just for the members of the organization but for the country. The potential is enormous. On the other side of the phone, I could feel her enthusiasm and excitement in making that announcement to me. "You have been one of the people who has really inspired me in this organization, and before making my announcement to run for national president, I wanted to inform you first." Angelica was already very active in her community in Panama City. Her family was involved in politics, and she had been very instrumental in opening doors for the organization in Panama City and the country as a whole. She was involved with the international organization, acting behind the scenes to host a series of international events in her city and offering her expertise in translations and event planning during international events. She already had the exposure and experience that anyone with ordinary narcissism would want. My question to Angelica was, "Why do you want to run for president?" Before she replied, I said to her, "If this is about the title and accolades, then I have no advice for you, but if this is about the young people of Panama, then we can talk." I paused, and there was silence on the other end. Then she said, "Thank you. I have to think about it and get back to you." Angelica never ran for president of her national organization but went on in her personal life to achieve great things for the young people of Panama, using her skills acquired in her active days within the international organizations and bringing her incredible connections in the city to support the organization. In other words, she did more without the title, and this was not for the benefit of one organization but the benefit of the people, particularly the young people of Panama. She confessed a few years later that the conversation she had with me changed her perspective. She was going to run for her own reasons and not for the reason that the organization existed, which was about creating opportunities that would empower young people to create positive change. Across the world in my seventeen years of extensive travel, I had found too many a leader take up positions for the wrong reason. Consumed by our own desire to willpower, maximize profits, earn admiration, or enjoy celebrity status, we sometimes fail to realize that we are called upon to start a business, exhibit our talent, or lead an organization because of the people—people who serve us or people whom we serve. Too often, we become blinded from the essence of our very existence—our mutual coexistence. It is all about people.

Coming from Africa, caring about people is rooted in the cultural beliefs of most of the African society. It is encapsulated in the now well-known philosophy of Ubuntu, "I am because you are." Without you, I am nothing. Long before the colonial influences, this philosophy has guided most societies across the world. It is not only African because in my travel across the world—learning about tribes in South America, the Native Americans, the Koreans, and Southeast Asian tribes—all observed this deep sense of our existence is dependent on others. At the core of the human spirit is our sense of existing because others exist.

CHAPTER SIX

Step Out of Yourself

There is more wisdom in listening than in speaking.
—African proverb

EACH TIME MY unofficial executive coach—my mother, Agnes Obenson—called me to find out how I was managing the stress of the workload, she would always say, "Quick to listen, not quick to talk." It had become so routine that I would finish the sentence as she started it. With her consistency, it actually became internalized. Those who know me know I am full of opinions—from politics to soccer and everything in between—but I learned over time and probably with the help of my mother's advice to listen to the opinions of others.

Sometime in March 2011, I was visiting a college on the outskirts of Colombo, the capital city of Sri Lanka, and I was asked to talk to some students about "impact." I left that experience having learned a lot more than I had shared. I wanted to know from the students why they had taken time to come out and listen to a strange African whom they knew and had heard nothing about. One of the students said something fascinating. He said, "I woke up this morning feeling very knowledgeable but no different than I felt yesterday and the day before. That knowledge means nothing if I keep it within. It makes a difference if I share it. I make somebody richer, but more importantly, I grow when I learn something new from someone—I get richer." As I write this book, I am grateful to that student although, regretfully, I do not have his name. He reminded me like my mother that it is not in listening to myself that I grow. In listening to others, we grow. We get the ability to absorb knowledge that did not come from within, and with every conversation, we have the ability to grow richer in knowledge.

Leading an international organization is tricky—especially in a very diverse world; different areas of the world had a different perspective on everything. The Europeans, who are by no means homogeneous, are very opinionated. The Africans are another very diverse group but culturally similar and typically keep their opinions to themselves until asked. The Asians always looked expressionless, have strong opinions, but toe the line with hierarchy irrespective of their personal opinions. The North Americans come across as the learned ones, they seem to have answers to every question and the emotional connection to build consensus (I am very surprised I just wrote that, mindful of everything that is happened under the leadership of President Trump). And then the South Americans almost mirror the Africans but are more political in nature. How do you lead in such a diverse world? Not simple at all, but listening helps. Traveling in Europe, I knew I had to listen. In Africa, I had to talk to get answers. In Asia, I went to the elders and asked for their blessing. While in South America, I needed a translator. In America, I had to be inspirational. Typically, when I did the rounds, I always ended up with a better solution, one that typically did not satisfy everyone but one that moved the organization forward. I learned that I had to step outside of myself—unless it crossed the lines of my values and the core mission of the organization. If I could sleep one night, it was a night that I found a solution that was middle of the road enough to please those in the middle and piss off those in the fringes of the spectrum of ideas.

Growing up as a member of JCI, I had joined what was known at the time as the Training Institute. This institute had been developed as a way to train trainers who could go out and evangelize about the organization. This institute grew extremely fast and almost consumed the organization. Those who became trainers could grow over time from a certified trainer to an international trainer. Over time, it was observed that the organization was becoming a training club. The organization was losing relevance in communities as more and more businesses invested in capacity building. I was a trainer. I was consumed in the fantasy world that by providing training to millions of young people, we could grow the organization and make it stronger—yet the reality of every passing year demonstrated the opposite. The more sophisticated young people, who were the quality of members needed to drive the economic engine of the organization, did not see value in our training since they could afford to attend the sessions of the John Maxwells of the world. We were, therefore, building an organization of the less talented. It was noble though to give them the skills, but most of these people did not seek to become members. They just came for the benefit of having access to a free or inexpensive learning experience and moved on. With numbers dwindling and quality on a downturn, the executive committee decided that the organization must take a different path. I was one of those who had a strong opinion to the contrary. I argued strongly that the training was relevant and that we should do more and help build the capacity of the less fortunate. However, in July 2012, the executive committee, made up of people of the key constituents of the world looking at the facts, had a different opinion. I had to step out of myself and wear the shoes and understanding of others to make a complete change in perspective. Being a leader, I changed my opinion, embraced a new direction, and even became the enemy of those who believed that classroom-style training was going to change the world. If it did, then with all the PhDs accorded to this date, there should not be any conflicts in the world. I learned and have argued since then that an entrepreneur is not one who takes one hundred hours of entrepreneurial courses but one who takes one hundred hours of trying to solve societal problems in a way that is financially sustainable. I learned and concluded that the best leaders are not those with hours of MBA leadership courses but those who start out as community organizers finding solutions to community challenges.

In 2006, I had traveled to South Africa as part of the work we were doing to build an organization that was representative of the indigenous people. Apartheid had ended in South Africa, but the hangover of it still existed. The JCI Organization in South Africa had been one of the most thriving in Africa but, since the collapse of the apartheid regime, had started to struggle as it was an essentially white organization. Mindful of the transformation of the country into a "rainbow nation," it was imperative that the organization reflect the diversity of the country. In 2004, the organization was suspended, following years of failure to transform, and I started working to rebuild a new national organization. I ran into a very dynamic lady called Tjibo Mathobi, who was well-connected and helped mobilize an indigenous population to relaunch a JCI in South Africa that was truly representative of the diverse nature of the country . . . or at least that was the hope. Well, during my visit in 2006, I found an organization that had gone from one spectrum of being very "white" to one that was very black. This did not represent the country either. Here I was a black man who wanted to see black Africans thrive, but thriving as a black organization was not my mission. I wanted an organization that truly represented the diverse nature of South Africa. In engaging the leaders of the organization, I found that they had all grown in the apartheid era and, to them, even imbibed with the values of the organization could not be objective enough to have an organization that included other races. I recall planning for a conference in 2007 and falling out with the national president at the time for insisting that a Jewish white boy who was local president speak at the opening ceremony of the Africa and Middle Eastern conference. These leaders did not have the ability to step out of themselves and see the bigger picture. I realized then that we had missed the biggest opportunity, one to build an organization that was truly inclusive. That for the years of oppression these young people had grown up with or seen, they could not bring themselves to be overtly open to those who oppressed them and benefit from the very organization that was meant to teach them to be tolerant of others.

Stepping out of yourself is detaching yourself from a deep-rooted notion. We must never assume that we are always right, for what is good at one point may not be good at another point. The history of the world is mired with this notion, from slavery to women's suffrage, equality to the gender pay gap, social security to maternity leave. Over time, these notions are seen to be the norm but are only changed when people have the ability to open their means to new perspectives—perspectives that lie ahead. There is a saying that that no one has ever prospered in the past. Prosperity lies ahead.

CHAPTER SEVEN

Pain of Change

However long the night, dawn will break.
—African proverb

BLACK DEVIL IS the name I acquired among the Cantonese-speaking Chinese in Hong Kong as I tried to build an organization that was more relevant to the world than to egos of a few out-of-touch back-seat drivers. I had learned very early on in life from a good friend, Thomas J. Clear III, to smile in the face of adversity. I was mindful that change does not come easy. If it did, then change will not be a struggle.

The history of the world is littered with heroic stories of transformation. The streets of cities and countries are stained with the blood of changemakers, and the corridors of governments soiled with the sweat of activists clamoring daily for a better world. So too—from boardroom to factory floor, soccer stadiums to production studios—are individuals who are standing up for not only their convictions but also their rights, advocating for just laws, calling for action on climate, standing for equality and pushing for economic opportunities for all. Change is hard. It comes at a cost, and people who fight for change end up with the scars—scars yes, but the triumph of change is the most gratifying.

In the summer of 2012, as Deputy Secretary General, I was the lead staff to a JCI event in Hong Kong. During these events, there usually was an awards ceremony. During this ceremony, the winners from an online entry judged by their peers were announced. As Deputy Secretary

General, I would receive the results typically the day before the ceremony. I usually kept it tight to my chest and even never wanted to look through the results so as not to be in any position to release the results beforehand. There had been rumors though that in Asia, the results were "fixed." It was, therefore, my mission to ensure that these results were as transparent and credible as possible. The day before the results, my colleague came to say that one of the influential past members of Hong Kong wanted to see the results before they were published. My response was that we must protect the integrity of the awards if we wanted the awards to mean anything, so we would not be sharing the results in advance of the ceremony. To my dismay, I was called into a meeting with the conference chairperson, Batbayar Ulziidelgar; two other influential past members of my organization in Hong Kong; and a dear colleague who was on the hot seat to produce the results. I politely said, "If this is the way things have been done in the past, the time has come for a change. The results will be announced tonight, and we will all find out." Needless to say, I had sown the seeds of hatred and earned myself the title of Black Devil (Hēi mówáng—黑魔王).

For nearly most of seventeen years, I've spent a lot of time traveling in Asia and particularly in Japan. I love Japan. I love the spirit on which that country is built. I appreciate and treat with reverence the Japanese culture, and I wish a lot more people could be exposed to it. The Japanese society is one that is very steeped in its rich culture. And what I find amazing is that Japan is a country that is very advanced in technology and at the same time a very traditional society. They have built a democratic society that is based on their traditional culture. They have woven technological advancement into the fabric of a three-thousand-year-old traditional society. That fascinates me. I have found great friendships in Japan, and I will also carry with me the memories of my over thirty visits to that country.

My first visit to Japan was in November 2004, and it was to the seaside city of Fukuoka. I spent nearly two weeks there refining my skills in eating raw fish—literally fished from a pond below the restaurant and sliced while still alive. I guess it strengthened our connection to nature, but surviving those days in Japan set me on the discovery of an incredible culture deeply rooted in our connection to nature. I also found a culture that even though advanced was still very closed to the rest of the world. I recall going out in the early morning to jog around the city, and by the third morning, I could see the people peering through their windows to see me jog. I found out it was quite uncommon for a black person to be seen in Fukuoka, and here was one jogging through their streets. They were extremely gracious and courteous . . . or at least that was how I felt. "Ohayō gozai masu!" They would scream out as I jogged past the early morning fish market shoppers. I also found out that the Japanese culture was very male dominated. Even as its young people were increasingly sophisticated and exposed to western cultures, they still defaulted to the age-old traditional society in which the women kept the home and the men took care of the business. This was not much different from the African traditions. The man was the breadwinner and protector of the family. The woman, she made sure the home was warm and the children healthy. This tradition still holds in most of Africa, but has been significantly eroded by the influence of western culture unlike in Japan. As I subsequently traveled to Japan in 2008 and then every year after that for eleven years, sometimes four times a year, I could see change happen, but it did so in a painfully slow manner.

In 2008, when I became executive director for growth, I asked myself where the opportunities for growth were within the organization. Japan was the leading market or national organization and had forty thousand members. To some, that was good enough. To me, I saw the potential of eighty thousand. Why? Ninety-seven percent of the membership of the organization was male and only 3 percent female. I could bet that there were young female Japanese women who were yearning to belong to networks like JCI and others. If we could open up the organization to women, we could easily increase our membership. How did I get it so wrong? There was a huge pushback. It was, in some quarters, even considered as offensive to Japanese. I learned a key lesson that I share with anyone who tries to do business in Japan. A good idea is not one that is announced on stage but one that receives the blessing of key stakeholders and is nurtured and embraced by the parties. Once an idea is embraced, you get unwavering commitment, and success is almost always guaranteed. You must, however, go through the painstaking process of consensus building.

Trying to grow the membership got pushback, but changing the conversation to the participation of women and later gender equality changed the dynamics. After our attempts to obtain the increase in female membership in JCI Japan failed, we resorted a push for more women to occupy leadership positions. In November 2015, at a congress in Kanazawa just as the United Nations had adopted Sustainable Development Goals (SDGs), JCI as an organization also adopted these goals. Of course, one of the overarching goals was equality and, particularly, goal 5: "Achieve gender equality and empower all women and girls." This was it! This was the opportunity that had taken years to achieve. In 2017, the oldest and second-largest local organization of JCI Japan elected its first female president in the name of Mami Hatano, and change was on its way. In 2019, under the leadership of JCI Japan president Takeaki Kamada, JCI Japan signed a memorandum of understanding with the government of Japan to promote the SDGs but particularly the SDG goal 5—"Achieve gender equality and empower all women and girls."

In February 2019, I was invited to Japan for its annual Kanazawa Conference that promoted the SDGs to moderate a panel discussion of gender equality. It was all women talking about their leadership role in business and society. It was a highly emotional moment for me. Change had come; it had been a long time coming. It was painfully slow, but it was here. Do I think the Japanese society is going to change overnight? Absolutely not. But the seeds of change have been sown, and it will come.

Change will always happen because society changes, and organizations, businesses, and countries have to change, or time will leave them behind. Leaders, visionary leaders, must be able to anticipate change and plan for it. There will always be resistance to change. The history of the world is full of such stories, but beyond the headlines of people who have changed the world are foot soldiers who fight every day to bring small changes in society that eventually lead to the bigger change. For example, Vanessa Nakate is a Ugandan climate activist who came to the limelight because she was cut out of a photo of a panel she was on with four white activists, and yet she had been leading climate change protests in Uganda for years, additionally, there are examples as the "Fees Must Fall". activists who brought free university education to students in South Africa. It takes times for change to happen.

Change is influenced by circumstances. In the case of Japan, the population is aging, and there is an increasing need for a young labor force, which can only be achieved through a significant increase in population. This obviously is not going to happen, so labor has to be imported, trained, and deployed. This will not happen soon and will be very expensive. Then comes the "eureka" thought—women. They are half the population and mostly staying at home. Investing in having women being treated as equal enables them to get out of the home to take up professional positions and grow into positions of influence. This all made sense, but it took years for them to come to the consensus that this was necessary.

Earlier in this book, I detailed how we took an organization that had been around for one hundred years but was little known and hardly relevant on the global scene and gave it a face-lift with a new mission, vision, and strategic positioning that made it become a player on the global scene. Everything we did was intended to build an organization that was resilient and that the world could turn to in times of crisis, like the coronavirus pandemic. We were doing not only what was right but also what was mandated to us after an extensive strategic planning process. But change can be intimidating. People fear change if they have a perceived threat to their interest. Such interest is typically not the interest of the organization or the business or even the country. Such threat is typically to the ego, to financial interest, to power play, and in some cases, to deep-rooted racial, religious, and tribal beliefs. Such interest is usually disguised in what will seem to be noble.

History tells us that the United States—despite the noble values laid out by its founders—is a country that went to war over slavery. Think of the United States torn between the North and the South because the people who had fled persecution and had fought for their very own independence against the British were at war because one part of the country wanted to continue to subjugate and rob fellow human beings of their dignity. Imagine how many lives and resources went to waste in the fight for independence that was based on an unsustainable premise of dehumanization. It was over two hundred years ago, and the United States still suffers the hangover of this awful past.

Nelson Mandela gave twenty-seven years of his life in his deep-rooted commitment to justice and equality. It was a cause worth fighting. Hundreds of thousands of South Africans lost their lives in the struggle for freedom. They were asking for something simple—to be recognized as human beings. It took nearly eighty years of struggle to win freedom at a great cost.

Change comes at great cost because people resist change. My experience with Japan helped me understand why people resist change. This was a unique experience because I could look at what was happening within the organization juxtaposed with what was happening in the society. There are several reasons why people resist change:

- *Information or misinformation.* People resist change either due to the lack of information or misinformation. Take the use of childhood vaccines, for example. Irrespective of what your position is, childhood vaccines have been 85 percent to 95 percent beneficial to recipients. This information is readily available, and medical history is full of praise of vaccines, and yet it just does not seem enough to convince the doubters about its benefits.

- *Fear of the unknown.* As human beings, we fear what we do not know. Take the internet, for example. Many of you readers may be too young to imagine a world without the internet, but there was a world without the internet. I started working using the in-and-out trays where letters came in either by mail or something called the fax. In 2002, my organization decided to go paperless, or at least that was the goal. With employees that had been there at work for decades, it was really hard for them to imagine a working environment that was going digital. In March of 2002, the organization moved location from Miami to Saint Louis, in the United States, losing 90 percent of its employees, and the new team of primarily young people were able to implement the change toward a paperless organization, a change that fifteen years later was still taking place.

- *Perceived threat.* People in position of power, or who are reaping benefits from the status quo, are typically resistant to change. Prior to the internet, my organization ran an awards program with projects submitted manually. These awards were judged by twelve to fifteen judges who were locked up in a room for two days. These people were segregated and spent most of their conference or congress reading through scrapbooks and arguing over which awards were better. However, it was observed that a pattern had emerged that those who could put together the most conspicuously beautiful scrapbook ended winning—even if the content of their project was not full of impact. Consequently, when we introduced the online award entries with a goal to level the playing field, there was huge pushback for those who felt they would lose dominance in the awards. Well, it was only a matter of time that these countries, typically the Asian countries, figured out that they could also submit outstanding entries online. The threat was perceived and not real.

- *Biases.* Sometimes people ignore the message because of deep-rooted biases against the messenger. Once I took a seat on the JCI Foundation, with fiduciary duties as secretary, I realized that for fifteen years, the principal of the endowment had been growing by nearly $400,000 (US dollars), and yet the interest generated for the organization had stayed the same. Anyone who understands what fiduciary duty means understands that as a board member, one has to act in the best interest of the fund. It was, therefore, a disservice to have an endowment that was not performing the purpose for which it was established—to generate revenue to support the organization. I, therefore, consulted with experts and developed a plan to grow the fund in such a way that it will still stay 80 percent conservative and 20 percent aggressive. Brilliant idea? Wrong! It was coming from a black African, not to be trusted. The Foundation Board asked for time to review it. Three years later, I put the same plan in the hands of a gray-haired white male, and it sold like ice cream on a scorching summer day. The resistance to change was based on deep-rooted biases. Through no fault of their own, they could not see past the messenger.

Understanding that there is bound to be resistance to change, one must be prepared to take the pain that comes with change. Whether it is changing digital processes, changing a business model, or fighting for justice, there will be resistance. Such resistance must be factored in our ability to stay the course and keep our eyes on the expected outcome. As we say in Africa, "However long the night last, dawn will break." Change will come.

CHAPTER EIGHT

The Chaos of Success

> When you have washed your hands, you can eat with the elders.
>
> —African proverb

OF ALL THE dreams we nurture and of all the plans we make, success comes like a thief in the night. You must have heard the saying, "Nothing goes by the plan." Success is hardly attained by the plan. Venture capitalists, investors, banks, board of directors, or even an electorate will demand detailed plans that demonstrate success, and it is logical to do so, but in reality, upon execution, the outcomes are usually very different. Success largely depends on a variety of circumstances, most of which we have touched on earlier in this book. But the world we live in is chaotic. The world is changing fast. What was obtained three years ago is not obtained today. In fact, what was obtained last year is not this year. Who would have thought that the hero of the year 2020 would be "online conferencing," but the pandemic came along, and our livelihood changed in ways we could not have imagined. Well, maybe science fiction did. Those who succeed, in the words of Jim Collins, do not thrive on chaos. But they can thrive in chaos."

> ***The Coca-Cola Company****, American corporation founded in 1892 and today engaged primarily in the manufacture and sale of syrup and concentrate for Coca-Cola, a sweetened carbonated beverage that is a cultural institution in the United States and a global symbol of American tastes. The company also produces and sells other soft drinks and citrus beverages. With more than 2,800 products available in more than 200 countries, Coca-Cola is the largest beverage manufacturer and distributor*

in the world and one of the largest corporations in the United States. Headquarters are in Atlanta, Georgia. (Culled from encyclopedia Britannica)

John Pemberton, an Atlanta pharmacist who founded the company, could not have imagined reading this in his wildest dreams. He had sought out to create a tonic for most common ailments at the time to be sold in local pharmacies. A year later, with success, he sold off portions of the business as a Griggs Candler, who registered the Coca-Cola trademark and grew the company phenomenally, and the rest is what we see today. Was Dr. John Pemberton the only creator of a magical tonic purporting to cure all ailments? In fact, in the 1890s and into the early 1900, all sorts of portions were being sold as miracle drugs, whether it is Stanley King and his snake oils or cocaine droplets sold for toothache by Lloyds Manufacturing Company and several other tonics that led to hundreds of thousands of addicts in the United States by the early 1900s, or even Bayer Pharmaceuticals' heroin-laced aspirin marketed for children with cough and cold symptoms. That was a tumultuous time in the world, no different than the times of the COVID-19 pandemic where people were finding solutions to endemic problems and turning to these tonics. Of the many, Coca-Cola, which was originally a combination and extract from the coca leaf and the kola nuts, thrived in that chaos to emerge as a drink with global repute. Today it is not even branded as a drink that sort of heals the body ailments. If anything, it is being frowned upon in certain quarters of doing damage to the body. The success of the Coca-Cola Company was chaotic because it could not have been imagined. The company has thrived in that chaos and continues to thrive because it has been able to reinvent itself to fit within the context of a fast-changing world.

Growing up in Cameroon, one of the supposed richest men in the country was called Victor Fotso. It was rumored that he started out as a street hawker selling peanuts. People always wondered how he could have gone from street hawking to being the country's first billionaire, owning prime property across the country, several manufacturing companies, and even opening the first independently owned bank in the country. Was he the only street hawker? Why did other street hawkers not grow to the same level of opulence like Victor Fotso did? What was it about him that he emerged? Well, for starters, it was not true that he started out by selling peanuts. In his book *Le chemin de Hiala* ("The Road to Hiala"), he recounts that he dropped out of school at the age of fifteen and started out working on farms growing cash crops like coffee and cocoa. He later opened up store branches in transportation, but his fortunes turn when he meets and forms a partnership with a French businessman Pierre Castel and invests in the importation of wines and spirits. Fotso continues to flourish, and through his relationship with another French man, Jacque Lacombe, he opens up a factory to produce matches. I am hoping now that as a reader, you are wondering first where Cameroon is and, second, who Victor Fotso is and why I am writing about him.

Victor Fotso's story to me is no different from the story of Dr. John Pemberton of the Coca-Cola Company and many other people around the world who started out with a goal of achieving one thing, and the chaos of success led them down a path beyond their imagination. Their success does not follow any logic of processes. It absolutely starts out with a thought process to solve a society problem or meet a need within the community, and because they had assembled a set of factors, circumstances lead them down a path of tremendous success. While we normally expect success to follow a certain logical process or pattern, in reality, success comes out of an illogical process that is chaotic at best.

In December 2018, my organization, in partnership with Africa 80, the African Parliament, and Global Citizen had successfully hosted an African Youth Development Summit in the sidelines of the massively successful Global Citizen Festival Mandela 100. The festival was organized by Global Citizen—an organization whose mission is quite audacious and impressive—to build a movement of one hundred million action-taking global citizens to help achieve our vision of ending extreme poverty by 2030. The festival was the first of its kind organized on African soil—Johannesburg—and dedicated to honoring the memory and works of President Nelson Mandela for South Africa.

I had been approached by Michael Sheldrick, Chief Policy and Government Affairs Officer, to engage young people to be involved with the movement and festival in celebration of the life of President Nelson Mandela. Global Citizen has built a movement out of a very interesting model. People are engaged in some form of advocacy, and with each action taken, an individual acquires points on their Social media platforms. These points are then converted into tickets for concerts around the world.

Faced with the opportunity, my team and I put on our thinking caps. Our goal was to focus not just on the organization but on how this opportunity could be offered to as many young Africans as possible. First, we focused on what we knew we were good at doing—empowering young people to create positive change. This meant we were not going to focus on members of our organization but on young people in general. We were expanding the pool to activists across Africa. This was accomplishing two things—giving the organization exposure to thousands of young people and, second, recruiting young people to join the organization. Second, we leveraged the power of collaboration by reaching out to other organizations of young people across the continent to partner with us on this endeavor. This led us to Africa 80, a group of young African global shapers, primarily entrepreneurs and activists who had authored a book titled *Africa 80: Transformation through Collaboration*. Thanks to the collaboration with Africa 80, we got connected to the African Parliament that became our principal sponsor. Working in collaboration, we developed a very exciting program. We developed a program targeting young African entrepreneurs who had started a business and/or activist below the age of thirty-five. In both cases, they had to be familiar with the Sustainable Development Goals (SDGs) and were either addressing some of the goals as part of their business model or activities within their communities. We put out a call for attendees, and within three days, we had more than 700 participants, yet we had room capacity for 150. Chaos ensued! How do we select 150 out of 700? How can we make sure the process is fair? How do we ensure a gender balance? How do we make sure every country is given a chance? What about the quality of the participants? These are problems we never envisaged. If anything, we thought it would have been a struggle to have participants to a workshop from across the African continent who would be paying for their travel and accommodation. Besides the quest for knowledge that was going to be obtained from the workshop, the only big incentive was the ticket to the festival. We dangled the ticket to the concert as a reward for completing two full days of the workshop. These were good challenges to have; even when I shared our success to the Global Citizens—the reason for the opportunity—it was hard to believe we pulled this off in less than two months.

The African Youth Development Summit was intended to be a side event of the Global Citizen Festival. It was listed on the overall program but really just another way to get African activists from around the continent to act. With the list narrowed down to two hundred, the event became the side attraction. UNICEF came in to partner with us. A National Geographic report who was recording a series called "Activate" came in to record the summit as an example of how the Global Citizen movement was built. Then there was the United Nations Deputy Secretary General, Amina Mohammed, who heard about the program and said she must attend, and then there was South Africa's biggest celebrity award-winning radio host TV presenter and style icon Bonang Matheba and then *CBS This Morning*'s cohost Gayle King, and the Reverend Al Sharpton. At some point, it was rumored that Oprah Winfrey was going to attend. Success is chaotic. We had a positive mindset, we focused on the opportunity, we were naively audaciously assembled, and we shared leadership with other partner organizations. These factors led us to hosting a highly successful African youth development summit. We built an army of young people across the African continent who committed themselves to mobilize fifty thousand young people to join an I Am Africa movement that would lead to the building of an Africa we wanted. These young people all joined the Global Citizen Movement and helped advocate for over seven billion dollars in commitments from African governments to end extreme poverty. Participants also got exposed to JCI, and well over seventy-five went on to become JCI members in their various countries.

This script could not have been written, and so is success. By focusing on what is possible and taking the right steps with the right mindset, one can achieve goals way beyond imagination. Any moment of doubt could change the trajectory. Focusing one's energy on challenges could also negate the outcome. In recounting this story, I never once mentioned that we had no funding, that we could not find hotels because they had all been booked, and that we only had two months to prepare for this event. Oh, did I mention that . . . even the president of my organization had absolutely no interest in this event and was shocked to see that it happened? Well, that is typical when anything is happening in Africa; the assumption is the worse. I can state that in seventeen years of planning and executing events around the world, not one has been as magical as this one was.

This side event also took the characteristics of the main event. The Global Citizen Festival that was beamed on television around the world as a musical was wildly successful and very chaotic too. On December 3, 2018, Neha Shah wrote on the *Global Citizen* blog an article captioned, "Global Citizens help fulfill Mandela's vision of ending extreme poverty by taking 5.6 million actions." This was just an incredible feat to achieve. When they started out planning this event in South Africa, they hardly imagined it would draw the amount of attention as it did. However, Global Citizen found the right hosting and presenting partner in the Motsepe Foundation, and together they brought the right set of actors to the table. For over a decade, I had been engaged with the Global Citizen, and for most who know this organization, they probably know the glamorous part of the organization. It is easy to see the spotlight, and yet this is an organization that has been in the making for many years. Hardly anyone realizes that its founders are from down under,

Australia, and with a clear vision and a positive mindset have found a way to make the fight against extreme poverty so cool that celebs around the world want to be associated with this organization. In my years of collaboration, I observed that they have an incredible ability to understand that success is chaotic and consequently are not intimidated by it. They have figured out that they are only as successful as their imagination can be stretched. They seem to understand that alone they may not be able to accomplish anything. They have developed a unique culture of collaborations, especially with the well-connected and famous.

Success is like rolling a boulder from the top to the bottom of a hill. Once one musters the energy and technique to unleash the boulder from the hilltop, it gains steam as it rolls downhill, taking with it any other items that may be in its path. Sometimes one will have to make really quick decisions downhill. In the same way, one assembles the right factors and gets an idea or project off the ground. Those ideas flourish only as a result of circumstances that arise and the decisions that one makes. I have coined this in my mind's eye as the boulder effect. The success of chaos is like the boulder effect. In Africa, it is said that once you have washed your hands, you can eat with elders. To get to success, there is a certain amount of chaos that you must accept as part of the business propositions. Things will not always go your way or follow the logical steps of your projections, but yet the persistence, the consistency, the mindset, the team, and most importantly, the quick decisions you make help you adjust and adapt to that chaos.

CHAPTER NINE

Bridging the Opportunity Gap

> If opportunity does not knock, build a door.
> —African proverb

THE TERM *OPPORTUNITY* according to Wikipedia has been used to connote two circumstances in business and in politics.

- in business, a market opportunity that a company or individual is not addressing

- in politics, a euphemism for a lack of equal opportunity

This book focuses on the former even though there are aspects of the latter that will be touched upon in this chapter. Business here is in reference to individuals, corporations big and small, associations big and small, and projects. The criteria here can be tested against project ideas. The essence here is really to give ideas the nourishing that will make them flourish.

The opportunity gap in my definition is the gap between where an idea, project, product, corporation, or country is and the potential of where it can be. It is the gap between the status quo and the future state. Bridging the opportunity gap has been used mostly in the United States to refer to the methods or pathways of closing the education gap between various segments of society or closing the inequality gap between the same. For purposes of this book, bridging the opportunity gap refers to the process of identifying the opportunities that lie within a society or business and deploying the right strategies to attain these opportunities. It can be applied as I have mentioned to individual talents, associations, movements, and countries.

For most of this book, we have focused on anecdotes from the past, but in this chapter, we will look to the future and apply some of the theories we have learned to ideas that can flourish.

Bridging the opportunity gap requires a mindset—a different mindset. We have overemphasized this mindset intentionally. We cannot build a prosperous future if we are so rigidly committed to the past. We must get rid of the elephant mentality. Elephants in the circus usually have a ring around a hind leg that is attached to a metal ball. When elephants are captured young, they are trained to stay within the diameter of the ring of the chain to the metal ball. The elephant grows to ten times its size, but because it has been trained to stay within the diameter of the ring of the chain to the metal ball, the elephant never thinks it can set itself free by pulling this metal ball that has a weight that is insignificant compared to the weight and force of the elephant. The elephant is so rigidly committed to its past that it does not explore opportunities in its future that are different from its past. We are typically so bogged down by our past experience that we almost become averse to exploring new opportunities. In 2005, mark my words, before the advent of Facebook, back in the days of something called Myspace, at my organization, we had created a very futuristic program called E-World. Think Facebook on steroids. It was meant to create a trusted community of business-minded young people collaborating to grow business ideas. Brilliant idea! However, it was only open to a few thousand people within the organization. In 2005, only a small fraction of the world was online. After several discussions with great friends that I must quote in this book as we worked in very close concert—Michael Kern and Zsolt Feher—we decided to propose to our board of directors to open up this program to anyone who was interested; it did not have to be a member-exclusive program. This was the source of a great deal of conversations that sometimes drew the passion akin only to a jealous spouse. "How dare we open this member benefit to nonmembers?"

These conversations were motivated by past experiences. This was a member-exclusive club, and we would rather keep it that way. Then Facebook went ballistic in 2006, and E-World choked to death because a community of ten thousand was no match to seven million at the time for Facebook. E-World died; we lost an opportunity because we were not open to a new way of thinking. We could have been the Facebook before Facebook. I learned a great deal from this experience.

As we look to the future, we must be mindful that the world is full of opportunity and that there is no idea too small to be transformational. In the same vein, there is no idea too big to be an obstacle for transformation. From our halls of government, the boardrooms of corporations, to the streets of communities across the world, we must embrace a future that is radically different from our past. This last statement may sound like cliché, but it has never been more relevant than now in a world post the new coronavirus pandemic. The pandemic has revealed that people can work remotely and leverage technology to generate billions in revenue. It has also demonstrated the incredible power that lies in the hands of people to inform and misinform. That in one day a video of a doctor and pastor peddling the efficacy of hydroxychloroquine as a cure for the COVID-19 could get twenty million views on YouTube and call into question the work of renowned clinical researchers and even get the attention, commentary, and participation in distribution by what used to be the most powerful position in the world—the president of the United States. As I write, the controversy rages on as the scientific community is thrown into confusion with a simple video. Not facts, not data, not a publication in a medical journal . . . just a video circulating on social media platforms. With or without the pandemic, the world seems to have reached the crossroads. Institutions of the world no longer seem to be responding to the aspirations of the people. Governments have become too gridlocked in philosophies instead of the governing and serving the purpose for which governments exist—maintaining order and security, protecting life, and ensuring the well-being of all its people. Corporations and the wealthy have become too invested in profit making that they rationalize the impact of their actions on the performance of the company stocks. It is amazing how the wealth gap continues to widen. In 2019, according to the Credit Suisse Global Wealth Report, the world's richest 1 percent—those with more than $1 million—owned 44 percent of the world's wealth. Nothing against the wealthy, but this is not a sustainable model, and something needs to be done to close the gap, without which it creates a phenomenal imbalance in society, leading to chaos. From the church to the civil society, organizations have become so philosophically divided that the essence of our presence here on earth, which is our collective survival, is compromised when one religion seeks to survive at the expense of another or one philosophy seeks to dominate to the exclusion of another. We have collectively as human beings placed our individual economic survival over our collective survival, and the consequences of that action are evident in the thousands who have died as a result of the coronavirus in the United States particularly, and across the world. Faced with a common enemy, we defaulted to our tribal instincts, leading to a patchwork response. Divided we fall has never been more apt a saying than now, where every country and, in some cases like in the United States, every state or city was left to their own devices to fight the coronavirus. The consequences have been disastrous. History will look back to this time in total dismay.

Despite the picture painted, the world's greatest opportunity lies in human life. Of all the things we sought to protect, we have the ability to create and destroy, be it the economies of the world, the educational systems, the stock market, the military, and all the precision artillery that we have so much invested in. All these things only exist because we have placed tremendous value in them. What we have not been able to create even as the book is written—there may be people trying to create one in laboratories unknown to the common man—is life. Human life! This is earth's biggest opportunity and the reason why bridging the opportunity gap is the most meaningful work we must embark on. The true purpose for every government, corporation, or association must be to serve, protect, and preserve life—be it human or nature.

The essence of this book and this chapter, in particular, is to foster an opportunity mindset that will lead individuals, corporations, associations, cities, and countries to bridge the opportunity gap. Bridging the opportunity gap will lift millions out of poverty, propel economies to grow faster, and transform the business landscape.

Take Africa, for example, as a continent—a continent that I have traveled extensively across. I have spent time with leaders across the continent, from heads of state to community leaders; encountered business leaders; and engaged with civil society actors. I have traveled to cities and villages; across muddy, swampy, and meandering roads; over mountains; and across valleys. And all I have seen is opportunity. Amid the challenges that the world sees projected on television screens and all over the internet lies an incredible potential for global economic transformation. It is the part of the world with the fastest-growing youth population, increasing educational level, a combined market potential of 1.2 billion, rising per capita income, and the world's fastest-growing economies despite the impact of the coronavirus pandemic. These factors alone tell me that the future lies in Africa. Sometime in early 2020, I reached out to an acquaintance from Switzerland, asking if he would be interested in speaking at an event in Africa. He asked me why I was organizing an event in Africa. "Why shouldn't I?" was my response. And he said, "Africa is poor. There is no money there." I got off that Zoom call utterly disappointed in the conversation. Africa is poor—that is the opportunity. Change that narrative, give them the ability to get out of poverty, and you will make money. Besides, it is incredibly senseless to think that Africans do not have money, yet their wealth has been plundered for nearly five hundred years.

In 2016, I met a Japanese gentleman in a very unusual setting. As I have said earlier, I traveled often to Japan, particularly in January, for a massive convention of Japanese men in black suits as I had observed the first time I visited. On this fateful trip though, I was invited to a dinner that was graced by the presence of the Japanese deputy prime minister, Taro Aso. As the leader of an organization that had over forty thousand members in Japan plus an alumnus of hundreds of thousands that for all intents and purposes ran the country, I was there to do what all leaders of nonprofit organizations do—beg for money. As is the case in Japanese culture, social events are where the bonds of trust are built. By social events, I mean sharing a drink or two or, well, several as the case may be. Sitting across from the table on the floor cushioned with pillows—a posture I struggled with enormously—Mr. Aso signaled to another gentleman to join us, and this became a transformational moment. I met Mr. Yusuke Saraya, CEO and president of Saraya Co. Ltd., a company you may not have heard of and probably will never hear of but one whose business model has been remarkably impressive. Operating in all continents across the world, Saraya Co. Ltd. was founded in 1952 and has grown to create a series of businesses that now include the development, manufacturing, and sales of health and hygiene products and services, consultation on food and environmental sanitation, as well as the development, manufacturing, and sales of food products. Mr. Yusuke Saraya, who also served as 1998 executive vice president for the JCI, has traveled the world extensively—both for business and for his passion for personal and community development. Since meeting Mr. Saraya, he agreed to sponsor two major international events, namely, the African Youth Development Summit in 2016 in the sideline of the Sixth Tokyo International Conference for African Development (TICAD VI) that took place in Nairobi, Kenya; and the African Youth Opportunity Forum that took place in Yokohama, Japan, in July of 2019 in the sideline of the Seventh Tokyo Conference for African Development (TICAD VII). This is important because his company really had no economic gain in sponsoring these series of events but for his conviction that by creating opportunities for the African youth population to be empowered, we can address the most complex challenges of our time. Over the last few years in my interaction with Mr. Saraya and his company, I have been inspired by his vision and business model. Saraya East Africa Co. Ltd. now owns a production facility in Kampala, Uganda, which is not ordinary for a company to have production facilities around the world. What I find fascinating is how the business was started in Uganda. It all started with Saraya joining forces with the government in a national handwashing campaign that was launched in 2007 in that country.

It is the notion of building the capacity of the local economy, creating a potential market, and consequently investing in partnership with the local economy that strikes me as transformational. Beyond the production of sanitary products, Mr. Saraya is invested in helping build the value chain for potential business opportunities. He is partnered with a local businessman in Kampala and opened up a Japanese restaurant in Kampala. Nothing extraordinary until you understand that Uganda is a landlocked country, and a Japanese restaurant needs fresh fish. He then created a value chain development program that sources fresh fish from local farmers or fishers in Nairobi and developed the technology to transport the same in good condition to Kampala, Uganda, a distance of about 660 kilometers. This is is what bridging the opportunity gap looks like.

Africa, as I have mentioned, represents tremendous potential for economic explosion if it is seen for the opportunity that it represents. Civil society organizations have played a key role in highlighting Africa's challenges for the last fifty years, but it is time to change that mindset and project Africa's opportunities. Instead of fighting against poverty, create opportunities for prosperity. Instead of fighting against corruption, build resilience and integrity. Instead of striving for gender parity, develop women leaders. By simply changing from coining the problem to coining the solution, we transform the approach and build a more attractive case for participation and funding. The same with every business initiative. Instead of looking at Africa as poor, as my Swiss friend concluded, we should look at Africa as a potential market, if we could lift four hundred million people out of extreme poverty in the next decade . . . Imagine how transformational that will be in economic value. The Unilevers, P&Gs, and Johnson & Johnsons of the world must be looking at Africa not just as a market to sell their products but as the future of the way their business will be structured. From labor to market, Africa will affect the future of every global business in ways that are unimaginable. The only way to be part of that unimaginable future is to invest now and play a role in that African transformation. Support the development of the social safety net across the continent, invest in capacity building, and develop the value chain of your current and future products. Have a stake in the development of the infrastructure, build a distribution pipeline, and help preserve the environment. This requires a massive transformation in the way these companies currently support development. This requires more than a token Corporate Social Responsibility (CSR) program. This requires being invested in the communities that they serve. This is beyond donations or programs designed for company employees. This cannot be a look good, feel good opportunity, it must be a deliberate and meaningful contribution to development. If I were consulted by big tech companies like the Amazon and Googles of the world, I would say to them, "Instead of selling the milk, own the goat." They do not just need to have representation in Africa, they must move to the future and embrace 1.2 billion opportunities and growth. It is time to create a partnership with the institutions to transform the educational system that will respond to the needs of future markets. This is the time to collaborate to build a pipeline of developers and skilled tech gurus for the next generation at a cost that is considerably lower than anywhere else. The investments of corporations big and small must be deliberate and not incidental to their primary businesses. It means leapfrogging Africa to a future where women do not have to burn wood to make meals for their families, with all the renewable energy options that are available. It means that we can keep freshwater lakes and rivers clean by revolutionizing waste management on the continent. African multinational institutions like the African Development Bank must revisit their current structures and embrace the civil society and the private sectors as partners in development. There must be a conscious effort not to address the status quo but to imagine a future that does not only address today's challenges but creates opportunities for tomorrow's generations. We cannot strive to create fifty million jobs for eight hundred million young people in a decade and hope that this will be sufficient. We must think bigger. We must strive to create one hundred million jobs each year for decades. This is possible because everything around Africa needs to be reimagined and reinvented. The World Bank must not fight poverty in Africa by relying on governments but must invest significantly in civil society and the private sector in ways that only the Marshall Plan has achieved in the past. Bridging the opportunity gap in Africa is bringing Africa up to par with the rest of the world; if that is not the case, Africa will always lag behind. We must build schools that have not been built anywhere else; put in place an educational system that is value based rather than certificate and employment-oriented, healthcare systems that are more oriented toward prevention than cure, and insurance that more rewards safety than disaster; have access to credit and investment policies that will stimulate creativity; reduce inequality; and accelerate economic growth. Africa is one huge market opportunity and must be looked at as such and not a patchwork of territories separated by colonially imposed boundaries that only continue to serve as an obstacle to unleashing the potential of this sleeping giant called Africa. We must leverage an army of eight hundred million young people representing over 60 percent of Africa's population to build a movement that will ignite a massive cultural shift and accelerate the biggest possible economic transformation in human history. It is this mindset that will bridge the widest opportunity gap that exists on earth today.

While I have used the example of Africa, this same mindset can be applied to every area of the world. From South America to Southeast Asia to the Middle East and Eastern Europe, the inequality gap can be closed by investing in massive capacity building and infrastructural development programs that will incentivize creativity, create jobs, and lead to prosperity. We have seen the result of China lifting hundreds of millions of people out of extreme poverty. Imagine the same in India and Thailand and Indonesia. I know what you are thinking . . . is this just some socialist or leftist ideology? No, it is not. It is a down payment for peace and prosperity. When the coronavirus pandemic hit the world, we saw governments around the world flood their economies with cash to keep those economies from collapsing. In the United

States, the Cares Act flooded $5 trillion into the economy, protecting jobs and industries. No one called this socialism or a leftist ideology since this was essentially spreading wealth around. Yet if we had gone to government leaders to propose a massive investment in capacity building and infrastructure development for just $2 trillion, it will be mission impossible. This exercise reveals that we have the resources to bridge the opportunity gap but sincerely lack the mindset and the will. We are rigidly committed to the past and find it hard to imagine a future unknown and different. Bridging the opportunity gap requires that we think wholesale rather than retail. The only way we move away from the challenges of today to a future that is prosperous is thinking wholesale; thinking big, bold, and audacious; and acting in ways where our action leads to massive transformation.

People talk about change, people are conscious that change will come, but they do so mostly to solve existing problems, and hardly do they envisage change that is radically different from what they have been used to. I recall in late 2018, after a major restructuring of the team of my organization, we decided to have four-day weeks, allowing for the employees to work from home on Fridays. We were not the first to start this, but to be honest, as the leader of an organization, I worried about level of productivity. For centuries, office space has been an integral part of work, but with technology and the coronavirus pandemic, we have another perspective of how people can work remotely. For nearly seventeen years, I traveled the world carrying with me a laptop and went from the dial-up internet to high speed (5G), and yet I always in my head felt I was out of the office. No—the office was always with me, in hotel rooms, conference rooms, coffee shops, airplanes, trains, and ferries. I have learned that bridging the opportunity gap is thinking beyond the ordinary, creating opportunities rather than addressing the status quo. I know I have repeated this over and over throughout this book. I will do so one more time—individuals, businesses, and organizations that focus on their challenges are defined by their challenges, while those that focus on their opportunities are defined by their opportunities. The way you move away from focusing on your challenges to focusing on your opportunities is through a mindset change—from one that is problem-solving oriented to one that is opportunity oriented. This is achieved through practice and experience to the point that it becomes second nature. After all, we are what we do repeatedly.

Bridging the opportunity gap requires that we stretch every idea to the limits of its possibilities. No idea is too small to change the world. I have come to learn that for an idea to flourish, it must be looked at within the context for key areas:

- Develop and implement a strategy.

- Build a movement.

- Keep your audience engaged.

- Embark on an advocacy.

These four key areas have informed my approach to every idea, and ideas have flourished or failed based on how I have applied each of these four key areas.

Develop and Implement a Strategy

The world is full of brilliant ideas and amazing theories that never get the legs to walk or wings to fly. Have you ever thought about a bright idea that you hold on to for a day, a week, a month, a year, and then it fades? Suddenly you see the same idea you had for days, weeks, months, and sometimes years being implemented by another person, and you look back and say to yourself, "I had that idea, but I just did not implement it." The difference between what you failed to do and what the other person did was strategy.

As recounted earlier, I am a veteran, having developed and implemented three strategic plans over ten years, from 2008 to 2018. Many people have the opportunity to be part of the process of developing or implementing a plan; few have had the experience leading a strategic planning process for an organization found in over one hundred countries, very diverse and mired in cultural and political differences. Prior to 2008, in 2004, I had been a member of the strategic planning committee whose plan stopped being implemented on the day it was adopted. That experience led to the conclusion that I hold today. A strategy is not a wish list of ideas but a well-thought process, which takes every idea, product, or philosophy from vision to reality. Strategy is a process; it must be deliberative, instructive, imaginative, and innovative. The outcome of strategy must inspire action, drive direction, and lay out a clear path to achieving the goals of an organization in the short and long term. Strategy alone is not enough; its implementation must be sacrosanct. Too often, organizations and corporations for that matter just check the box and are not committed to the plans they develop. There must be the will to implement, and it must be understood all through the organization. Whether it is a small or large organization, their strategy must be adopted in such a way that it informs every decision that is being made by the organization. Everything must be filtered through the lens of the strategic plan and anything that does not fit within the context of lens, the organization must stop doing or refrain from doing. This is not a walk in the park. It requires discipline, coherent and unwavering commitment.

My experience has shown that strategy must be based on a philosophy. I have come to learn about three of such philosophies that have guided my development and implementation of strategy. These philosophies are embodied in three key questions to be asked that will drive the direction of every strategy.

- What is your purpose?

- What do you want to be the best at?

- How will you be different?

What Is Your Purpose?

Earlier in this book, I recounted the herculean effort we had made in redefining the mission and vision of the organization. We had realized that an organization that was everything to everyone was, in the end, not serving its purpose. Purpose is the reason for which your organization is created or the reason why it exists. Defining the reason for which you exist is very important as it lays down the foundation upon which to build the organization. To answer that question, you must ask why you want to or are doing what you do. Over the years, as I have dealt with changing boards of directors and staff, I used the work of Simon Sinek—particularly a video based on his book *Start with Why*.

Interesting that I found this video nearly three years after we had gone through the process of focusing on the why of our organization, and his work came to lend credence to what we sought to accomplish.

Simon Sinek states that "People do not buy what you do, they buy why you do it." Understanding and communicating effectively why you exist serve as a good way to attract people to your movement, organization, or even business.

As the world changes and people are becoming a lot more drawn to values of individuals, products, or organizations, understanding your "why" and purpose is of great importance. Defining your purpose will lead you down a path of developing a vision statement and a mission statement for your organization. It does not matter what sector your organization is in; it does not matter how young or how old your organization is. What matters is that you clearly understand why your organization exists.

I, therefore, recommend starting with asking "why" as you develop a strategy for your organization.

What Do You Want to Be the Best At?

In 2008, when tasked with developing a strategic plan for my organization at the time, I knew that I needed expert help. After several consultations, I met a gentleman called Johnathan Jones, whom I must give credit for introducing me to the work of Jim Collins. I have been inspired particularly by the books *Good to Great* and *Built to Last*. I will recommend these works to every organization that is seeking to devise its strategy. Since learning about the work of Jim Collins, I have drawn inspiration from his work, particularly something called "the hedgehog concept."

The hedgehog concept originates from a Greek parable and is accentuated upon by the author, Isaiah Berlin in his *The Hedgehog and the Fox*, in which he divided the world into hedgehogs and foxes. This further inspired Jim Collins to develop "the hedgehog concept." The ancient Greek parable says, "The fox knows many things, but the hedgehog knows one big thing." While the fox is known for being a fast, cunning, cute, and sleek animal, the hedgehog is known for just one thing—its ability to defend itself. The fox uses all sorts of tricks and techniques to catch the hedgehog but ends up all the time with a bloodied nose from the quills of the hedgehog. This parable seems to resonate with me, probably because this is how knowledge is transferred in Africa by way of anecdotal tales. There are hundreds of African stories that can be told in such ways. For example, "A good hunter is not known from how many wrestling matches he wins but from the game he brings home."

The one thing you are best in the world at doing is what you are passionate about. It is your reason for being; in other words, what you are best at doing is informed by your purpose. When people ask me for advice about what field they should go in to study, I ask them what they are passionate about. I grew up in a country and with parents who wanted the outcome for their children to be a lawyer and doctor, nothing more and nothing less, but none of that was driven by passion. Instead, our parents wanted for us a successful life in which we could earn a living and contribute to society. Here I am, a lawyer, writing a book and that is not legal submission, after having spent most of my adult life traveling the world and inspiring young people to become actors rather than spectators in their destiny. I do not tell students to pursue a profession that makes the most money; I typically advise them to follow their passion. In following your passion, you excel. When I sat in interviews with potential team members, I always said to them that, "if you are looking for a job to earn a living, look somewhere else, but if you are seeking a purpose, then I have a mission for you.".

Finding what you are passionate about and determining how you can develop a sustainable living out of it is a sweet spot that every individual, organization, or association should be in. Determining how sustainable your passion can be is significantly dependent on its relevance to the wider society. If your passion solves a challenge in society or adds value to people's lives, you are likely to make that passion economically sustainable. Jim Collins coins that as your "economic engine."

How Will You Be Different?

Every day, there is a continuous race for people's attention. From the mainstream media to social media, people are devouring an unfathomable amount of information. From sunrise to sunset, people are accessible—in bed, in the bathrooms, at the breakfast table, on the drive to work, at work, at lunch, at dinner, and back to bed. We have become increasingly attached to the group chats, catching up with old friends, debating conspiracy theories, and forwarding all sorts of outrageous memes. With so much struggle for attention, the only way to get the attention of people is to stand out. Stand up and stand out!

Imagine this for a moment; a traditional classroom (I mean what used to be the traditional classroom), where there are twenty students (well, I come from Africa, and my classroom size was forty-eight). In this classroom, there is a teacher who stands in front of the classroom, so he gets everyone's attention even without speaking. When he asks a question and the students all know the answer, they all shout it out. The next time he asks a question, he requires a student to stand up and go to the front of the classroom to give the answer. Which of these two responses will the nineteen or forty-seven other students actually remember? Of course, it will be the student who stood up and stood out. Enough of that traditional setting; let's get back to the future.

Over the years, marketing and advertising firms have sought to stand out, to be different not in the products but to get the attention of consumers. Looking to the future, it does not suffice to stand out, but you must stand up. Standing up means demonstrating you represent something of great value. Do not just be an organization; be an organization that stands for something. Do not just be a membership association for accountants; be an association that upholds the ethics of good accounting practices. Do not just be a bicycle rental company but be one that promotes safe bicycle riding. Do not just be an e-commerce company but be one that is invested in protecting the privacy of consumers. Do not just be an investment firm but be one that is investing in building a more sustainable society. Do not just be a college but be one that is building active citizens who will, in turn, build a better society. Organizations must find ways to strike a chord with the trending values of its stakeholders. Being different means that you position your organization to be part of the livelihood of its stakeholders.

There are various schools of thought on what strategy is. I have shared the three things that have animated my experience in strategy development. The most important thing to retain is that strategy will give you direction. It is intended to move your organization toward its vision over a period of time. As I mentioned earlier, strategy is not just for the big organizations; it is for everyone. Smaller organizations sometimes do not see value in investing to develop a solid strategy. It is a struggle between investing resources in strategy development as opposed to investing in the business. It is such a paradox to think that investing in the strategy is not investing in the business. Strategy must become an integral part of the business if that business must grow. I, however, understand this struggle from leading an organization where people, interestingly, even on the board of directors, did not see value in investing in strategy for an organization of global dimension. It, however, is very necessary for the survival of every organization. Failing to have a strategy is failing to succeed. Without clear choices about the direction of your organization, it is like navigating a ship without a destination.

Having clear choices for the direction of your organization means having clear strategies. Not tactics but strategies. Strategies are a set of overarching goals while tactics are the action steps to be taken. Strategies are not achieved overnight; they are implemented deliberately over a period of time. Tactics are the short-term action that needs to be taken to achieve each goal. For example, we decided that our organization needed a new mission. Upon adoption of the new mission, we needed tactics for the implementation of the new mission. We insisted that the mission be recited at every meeting with the words projected on a screen. We created sample banners for download with the mission, allowing local organizations across the world to print them locally and have them in their meeting rooms. In less than five years, there was a 100 percent adoption of the mission in over one hundred countries and nearly five thousand cities. Incredible! Strategy and tactics are complementary. The one must go with the other. It was the Chinese military general Sun Tzu who said, "Strategy without tactics is the slowest route to victory. Tactics without strategy are the noise before defeat."

Finally, strategy only works if it is implemented. It requires discipline and commitment. Organizations invest stupendous sums of money to develop strategies, they organize focus groups, surveys, workshops, and forums, only for such strategies to end up in great presentations, binders, and folders. The purpose of a strategy is to drive direction. That only happens when the people affected by the strategy take ownership of it. They own it; they make it happen. Organizations must designate what is now commonly known as a chief strategy officer who is the guarantor of the implementation of a strategic plan. Such a person holds the organization accountable for implementation of the plan and justifies that investment in the plan. The strategy itself must determine how it will be implemented throughout the organization. I have always said a good strategy is not one that is remembered line by line by the stakeholders of the organization but one that informs every action of its stakeholders. I look back with great pride to see that our strategies have inspired historic action like World Clean Up Day by the Let's Do It Foundation, or the campaigns like the Peace Is Possible Campaign or the I Am Africa Movement and many other campaigns that are being run across the world. Strategy will inspire achievements that are unimaginable at the time of conception. Strategy will bridge the opportunity gap between your current state and your potential state. It will bridge the opportunity gap between your idea and your potential achievements.

Build a Movement

In a fast-paced world where everyone is vying for attention, lone voices, no matter how powerful, cannot make a difference. It's the mobilization of people with common social, economic, or political interest that makes a difference. In today's world, for any idea to flourish, one must carve out a community, generate interest, empower, and incentivize action. It used to be that movements were thought of as only for activists and politicians. However, nowadays and going forward, for an organization to grow and flourish, it has to build a movement around its purpose. It must think about itself as a movement.

The essence of thinking like a movement generates interest and creates opportunities for growth. In today's world, with available technology, we have the ability to communicate with people outside the traditional networks. We must think of ourselves, our products, and organizations as mobile billboards that can be read at every corner of the world that technology permits. We are no longer limited by the boundaries and national regulations in the way that previous generations were.

Everything we do today has the potential of building a movement around it. A movement will facilitate positioning, increase awareness, and cut through the noisy distractions of everyday life. A movement will bridge the opportunity gap. It will take an idea, organization, or business from its current state to achieving its greatest potential.

A bank can build a movement not just of its customers but potential customers. This movement can leverage the engagement of its members to define access to credit, understand, and drive consumer trends as well as influence policy change. A membership organization can build a movement that tends around its purpose and position itself as relevant not only to its members but also to the communities in which its members belong by influencing change in those communities. Even a business producing a product as unsexy as nails used for construction and building must build movement of nail users that ensure the safe usage of building products, teach its audience about how to use nails, and learn more about how its products can be safe. A government can build a movement of young people and leverage the voices and input of young people to develop progressive policies of the future.

To bridge the opportunity gap, we must think beyond the ordinary. Ordinary is what it is—ordinary. A movement takes an ordinary organization to an extraordinary one. A movement will bridge the opportunity gap.

Keep Your Audience Engaged

Building a movement is like building a tent and inviting the neighbors over. Once that tent begins to fill up, there must be activities going on that will keep people inside, without which they will slip out to the next tent and then to the next tent. In the new world we live in, we must think about engagement in the same way we think about engagement within the context of an audience in a room. People will check out if you do not keep their attention. When they check out, their attention will go somewhere else. There is nothing like overengagement. If people feel overwhelmed, then it is what you are doing that turns them off. What is your story? Tell it as many times in various ways. What are your values? Do they align with those of your audience? Show them. How do you want your audience to act? Show them and challenge them to do the same. Be a center of knowledge; people want to learn something new, so feed them with knowledge. Create opportunities for constant engagement; use events whether digital or in person as a way to communicate directly with your audience.

I have mentioned earlier about an international peace summit that we organized in Kuching, Sarawak, Malaysia, in 2017, drawing the attendance of nearly eight hundred activists from thirty-two organizations around the world. As a prelude to this summit, we ran a global campaign called Peace Is Possible the previous year, and with this campaign on September 21, we engaged four million people, who made commitments to peace. We built the tent, we established credibility, and the following year, we created an international summit to continue engaging that audience. It is noteworthy that we were running an organization of nearly two hundred thousand people, and yet we were able to reach four million people and attract thirty-two other organizations to our campaigns and summit respectively. We equally had other forms of engagement, notably six activities that people around the world could do to contribute to peace. In six months, there were activities in well over eighty countries. I will never forget seeing the images of a peace march in war-torn Aleppo, Syria, and thinking how amazing what a simple idea could do to change the world. We started out with a strategy, built a movement, and we kept the movement engaged.

Embark on Advocacy

An empowered audience can wield transformative power. Organizations spend huge sums of money on lobbyists to affect changes in policies or maintain the status quo. Organizations typically work with lobbyists to protect their interest. Lobbying as a trade typically is not seen in a positive light. The trade is perceived as opaque. However, lobbying takes place every day and everywhere whether regulated or unregulated. It is the massive sums of money that change hands that make it questionable. As organizations begin to build movements of engaged audiences, they will have to capitalize on these audiences to affect the kind of change they will like to see. Take, for example, the Saraya Co. Ltd., which I mentioned earlier. They source raw materials from Malaysia, notably palm oil, and because the planting of palm oil means that huge areas of forest need to be exploited, it has an impact on the elephant population. The Saraya Company has now become an advocate for wildlife conservation, investing significantly in this area. Going forward, the Saraya Company can engage the consumers of its products to become advocates of wildlife conservation, asking them to contribute financially or charge their legislature to create policies that will support or encourage wildlife conservation.

With the rapid technological advancement, consumers will only continue to wield incredible power. In their hands will lie the success or failure of millions of products, the future of organizations, and the destinies of countries . . . and dare I say, the human race. Organizations that understand and capitalize on this using these four pillars to bridge the opportunity gap will succeed. The playing field is levelled, but the path to navigate through it will demand a well-crafted strategy.

Bridging the opportunity gap is a philosophy rooted in the simple belief that by focusing on what is possible, one can achieve it. It is harnessing opportunities that have the potential of transforming the world. The world is full of people with incredibly innovative ideas that can be transformational for mankind. Too many of such ideas die because these dreamers see or are met only by obstacles in their way. But as the world is changing—rapidly—the traditional economies will no longer be able to cope with the aspirations of new generations that are yearning for adventures that go beyond the confines and contours of national boundaries. These next generations, call them whatever letter you choose, will increasingly see the world differently from the way boomers, Gen Xers, and the millennials see it. The world must brace itself for a transformation that is beyond our comprehension. The only way to mitigate the impact of this massive transformation that is about to come upon the world is to bridge the opportunity gap.

A few years ago, while serving on the board of the Ban Ki-moon Centre for Global Citizenship, I was honored to be asked to record and teach a course on global citizenship. Unsure of what to teach, I spent weeks consuming any literature on global citizenship I could find. I was amazed by what I uncovered. Since the first ships set sail out of Europe, rounding the West African coast by the Portuguese in the early 1400s as it was written in history, it sparked a movement toward globalization that continues today. That movement has faced upheavals but has largely moved forward, connecting the world with every passing year. True to human nature, the movement toward globalization has been constrained by our tribal instinct; as human beings, we have sought to protect our own against the unknown or sought to conquer and dominate the weak. Conflicts and eventual control of territories have ensued, then the notions of states, the fight for independence, and the eventual recognition that human beings were born equal. All these upheavals have been trumped by our interdependence. Human beings have always been in search for opportunities that will make life better. While we live in a world that is far advanced from what it was when those sailors set sail into the largely unknown world, the human desire of searching for greener pastures or opportunities continues and will continue irrespective of the walls or bridges that we build. While these human movements may not be as glamourous as the days of the Bartholomew Diazes, they certainly are as adventurous. Take the movement of economic refugees from Africa crossing the Mediterranean Sea and the thousands who die in the process. Take the movement of economic migrants from South America marching to North America, despite the treacherous terrain. These movements may be seen from a sociopolitical prism, but they have an enormous socioeconomic impact both in the North and the South that will transform the future of the world in ways that we cannot conceive at this time. It also largely demonstrates a phenomenal gap in human progress even as we agree that all human beings are born equal but, obviously, unequal in opportunity.

I learned from teaching a global citizenship course that because we live on planet earth and because we are increasingly interconnected and interdependent, we have challenges that can no longer be redressed within the framework of national boundaries. From climate change to human trafficking, poverty to human rights, or the economy to education, all these issues that were once only addressed within the frame of a country or treaty are now understood to affect the world much more broadly, beyond man-made boundaries. The world must think anew.

The world needs a mindset that is more proactive than reactionary. We need to develop a next generation that does not seek to perpetuate the status quo or strive to attain today's reality but one that can consciously and conscientiously design its future to be more inclusive, more prosperous, and more ecologically sustainable. This is a mindset that can be developed in individuals, in organizations, in governments, and why not on a global scale?

You must be thinking, *such a dreamer*. How can this even be possible? Make no mistake. I understand that there will be failures and setbacks. I understand that the path to success—any success—is incredibly arduous, but I know for certain that there is room for growth and expansion when we focus on what is possible as opposed to what is impossible. I know that if we focus on our opportunities, we will be defined by opportunities. We can build a world that is defined by our opportunities. It starts by simply changing the way we think. For example, instead of fighting against poverty, let us focus on creating prosperity for millions. Instead of climate change, let us focus on sustainable living. Instead of fighting illiteracy, how about giving every human being the ability to reach their greatest potential? Just a few examples of how we can upset the paradigm and then begin to work toward it. We can achieve all these things, as ambitious as they may sound, if we fix our minds to it. We, as the human race have only achieved the things that we fixed our minds to.

Everything that I have shared with you so far comes from what I have experienced and researched and of which I deeply and passionately believe. In nearly a half century of my lifetime—a lifetime that has been rich in experience, full of setbacks and wins—I have always been impatient for change, but that impatience has run out. I have to conclude that the only thing that stands in the way of change is the human mind. I know deeply that the human mind is capable of amazing imaginations and achievements; it is also capable of creating monstrous barriers. I have observed that the mind can be trained to see possibilities rather than impossibilities. That what the mind is trained to believe, it will. What the mind believes, it can bring the body to achieve. I also know that the pace of evolution of our economies, our institutions, is lagging behind what we are humanly capable of. The world needs a catalyst! It needs people like you thinking and acting differently, embracing a future that is beyond comprehension. It is the ability to embrace such unconceivable future that thankfully brought us the internet, that took us to the moon and back, that lifted over five hundred million out of extreme poverty in a decade, and that has seen the fastest wealth creation in human history.

Consequently, I hope this book inspires possibilities and triggers action. I hope you pause at this point and look back at how you have approached issues as an individual. Have you been focusing on opportunities, or have you been focusing on challenges? Do you lead an organization or run a business? How have you interacted with your team or board of directors, employees, or members? Are you an activist, wanting to lead a movement to change something? What has been your approach to demanding change? A small business with a brilliant idea but facing headwinds, how are you going about developing your strategy? What philosophy are you adopting? Do you have the ambition to run for office? Are you cataloging problems, or are you offering solutions that will leapfrog your community or country? Are you the head of a family, a household, a sister, or a brother? How are you dealing with challenges? Are you bogged down by generational disputes, or are you facing the future with great optimism? I sincerely hope that we can spark a movement about how we think about the future. A movement where we can look at the world not as it is today but elect to design a world for what it ought to be based on the values that animate us. I invite you to join us in "bridging the opportunity gap." I invite you to join this movement; share your ideas, thoughts, and experiences; and let us go on a journey of transformation—one individual at a time, one organization, one community, one country, and let this movement become a catalyst for change.

Let me end with these words: if you were given a canvas to paint a future, would you paint it all dark and gloomy, or will you paint it all colorful and bright? The destiny of the world is in your hands, and with every stroke of the paintbrush, you give the color and the sensation you want. What will be your choice?

The End!

INDEX

A

Abang Abdul Rahman Zohari Abang Openg, 60
Africa, 2, 6, 28, 47, 73, 84–85, 90, 92, 94
Africa 80, *81*, *82*
African Development Bank, 93
African National Congress, 59
African Parliament, 81–82
African Youth Development Summit, 83
Alcoa, 43–44
Alufohai, Desmond, 25
Amazon, 4–5
Asia, 67, 72
Aso, Taro, 90

B

Berlin, Isaiah
   The Hedgehog and the Fox, 99
big-picture thinking, 41–46, 50–51
boulder effect, 85
Buthelezi, Mangosuthu, 59

C

Cameroon, xi, 6, 10, 25, 39, 48–50, 81
   development of, 48, 50
Cares Act, 95
Chadwick, Florence, 5
Coca-Cola Company, 79–80
collective survival, 89
Collins, Jim, 8, 13–15, 79, 99–100
   Good to Great, 8, 14, 99
   Great by Choice, 14

committee
   executive, 68
   strategic planning, 9, 14, 16, 21, 97
coronavirus, 39, 50, 89, 94–95
corporations, 4, 61, 88, 97
   investments of, 93
corruption, 49
credits, 28, 94
Crutchfield, Leslie
   Forces for Good, 21

D

Duhigg, Charles
   The Power of Habit, 44

E

education, 62
elephant mentality, 87
E-World, 87–88

F

Facebook, 87–88
Factfulness (Rosling), 1
Forces for Good (Crutchfield and Grant), 21
Fotso, Victor, 80–81
   Le chemin de Hiala, 81

G

Global Citizens, 81–82, 84
Global Youth Empowerment Fund, 20
Goldsmith, Marshall, 53

111

Good to Great (Collins), 8, 14, 99
Grant, Heather Mcleod
    Forces for Good, 21
Great by Choice (Collins), 14

H

Hammamet (Tunisia), 2–3
Hedgehog and the Fox, The (Berlin), 99
hedgehog concept, 99
Holmes, Elizabeth, 35–36
Hougaard, Rasmus, 63
Hutu, 6

I

I Am Africa, 83, 103
I Am Cameroon, 50
impact, 11, 17, 20–21, 66
    sustainable, 18
Indomitable Lions, 6
internet, 77
Irish Times, 59
Isidore, Chris, 4

J

Japan, 72–76, 90–91
    culture of, 72–73, 91
    government of, 74
JCI (Junior Chamber International), xi–xii, 13, 17, 19–21, 25, 33, 38, 67, 74
JCI Active Citizen Framework, 11–14, 17, 42
JCI Japan, 74
JCI South Africa, 69

K

Kennedy, John Fitzgerald, 29
Kodama, Edson, 2
Kuching (Sarawak), 60, 105

L

Lam, Angelica, 64
leadership, xi, 38, 52–53, 55
    politics of, 7
    solitude of, 53–54
Limbe General Hospital, 24, 26, 28

M

Maktoum, Mohammed bin Rashid al-, 50
Mandela, Nelson, 58–59
Marriott, Alice, 63
Marriott, J. W., 63
Marriott International, 63
marshmallow test, 41
Mathobi, Tjibo, 69
Middle East, 50

N

naive audacity, 25, 28, 30–31, 34–38, 40
Nakate, Vanessa, 75

O

Obama, Barack, 37
One Rwanda, 6
O'Niel, Paul, 43
opportunity, 104
Opportunity Gap, 86–87, 94–95, 104, 107
opportunity mindset, 7, 14, 23, 52, 90
organization, 1, 3–4, 7, 9, 13, 18, 20, 22, 42, 53–54, 56, 97, 101, 103, 105–6
    mission of the, 55, 98
    nonprofit, 22, 91
    strengths of the, 12

P

Panama, 64
Peace Is Possible, 20, 103, 105
Pemberton, John, 80–81
Power of Habit, The (Duhigg), 44

R

Rosling, Hans
   Factfulness, 1
Rwanda, 6
Rwandan Patriotic Front, 6

S

Sarawak, 60, 105
Saraya, Yusuke, 91
Saraya Company, 91, 106
SDGs (Sustainable Development Goals), 20, 74, 82
Sears, 4–5
Shah, Neha, 84

Sheldrick, Michael, 82
Sinek, Simon, 98
South Africa, 42, 68–69, 83–84
Suzuki, Severn, 32–33

T

Theranos, 35–36
Thompson, Derek, 4
Thunberg, Greta, 33–34
Transformunity, xii
Trump, Donald John, 37

U

Uganda, 91–92
United Nations, 21, 74

W

Wagner, Rodd, 43
World Cup, 6

CPSIA information can be obtained
at www.ICGtesting.com
Printed in the USA
LVHW031604250521
688466LV00003B/563